Practical Spiritual Gifts

James W. Zackrison

Pacific Press Publishing Association
Boise, Idaho

Edited by Ken McFarland
Cover photo by Lars Justinen
Type set in 10/12 New Century Schoolbook

ISBN 0-8163-1357-1

96 97 98 99 00 • 5 4 3 2 1

Contents

Introduction

Since 1980, the Seventh-day Adventist church has included a declaration about spiritual gifts in its statement of 27 fundamental beliefs:

"God bestows upon all members of His church in every age spiritual gifts which each employ in loving ministry for the common good of the church and of humanity. Given by the agency of the Holy Spirit, who apportions to each member as He wills, the gifts provide all abilities and ministries needed by the church to fulfill its divinely ordained functions. According to the Scriptures, these gifts include such ministries as faith, healing, prophecy, proclamation, teaching, administration, reconciliation, compassion, and self-sacrificing service and charity for the help and encouragement of people. Some members are called of God and endowed by the Spirit for functions recognized by the church in pastoral, evangelistic, apostolic, and teaching ministries particularly needed to equip members for service, to build up the church to spiritual maturity, and to foster unity of the faith and knowledge of God. When members employ these spiritual gifts as faithful stewards of God's varied grace, the church is protected from the destructive influence of false doctrine, grows with a growth that is from God, and is built up in faith and love." *Fundamental Belief*, No. 16.

The continuing application of the gift of prophecy in the person of Ellen White has always been part of the Seventh-day Adventist belief system. The rest of the spiritual gifts mentioned or alluded to in the New Testament have not had as high a profile until recently.

Nevertheless, the New Testament indicates that it is through the assignment of spiritual gifts that the Holy Spirit designs to carry out the work of the church. The apostle Paul outlines the spiritual gifts system in Rom. 12, 1 Cor. 12–14, and Eph. 4. From these passages, and from illustrations of giftedness in people's lives, it is possible to construct a workable plan for the utilization of spiritual gifts in the life of the church.

The identification and application of spiritual giftedness is not an exact science. It is a subset of the overall meaning and application of discipleship by the individual member and the congregation as a whole. This book is an attempt to follow the advice of Paul: "Now about spiritual gifts brothers, I do not want you to be ignorant" (1 Cor. 12:1). It examines twenty-seven spiritual gifts named or alluded to in the New Testament.There may be more than these twenty-seven, but they are the primary ones mentioned in the Bible.

Identifying and employing your spiritual gifts in ministry will enhance your personal religious life and the life of the congregation of which you are a part—and give real meaning to Paul's message that we serve as ambassadors of the King of Kings (2 Cor. 5:17-21).

ONE

Introduction to Spiritual Gifts

William McRae tells about an advertisement of a job offer for a pastor. It read in part: "WANTED: Minister for a Growing Church. A real challenge for the right man!

"Applicant must offer experience as a shop worker, office manager, educator (all levels, including college), artist, salesman, diplomat, writer, theologian, politician, children's worker, psychologist, funeral director, missionary, wedding consultant. Must know all about problems of birth, marriage, and death. Must be forthright but flexible; return criticism and backbiting with Christian love and forgiveness.

"Should have outgoing, friendly disposition at all times. Should be captivating speaker and intent listener. Education must be beyond Ph.D. requirements but always concealed in homespun modesty and folksy talk. Must be willing to work long hours, subject to call any time day or night, adaptable to sudden interruption. Will spend at least 25 hours preparing sermon. Additional 10 hours reading books and magazines.

"Applicant's wife must be both stunning and plain, smartly attired but conservative in appearance, gracious and able to get along with everyone. Must be willing to work in church kitchen, teach Sunday School, babysit, run the copier, wait table, never listen to gossip, never become discouraged.

"Opportunity for applicant to live close to work. Furnished home provided; open-door hospitality enforced. Must be ever mindful the house does not belong to him. Directly responsible for views and conduct to all church members and visitors, not confined to direction or support from any one person. Salary not commensurate with experience or need; no overtime pay. All replies kept confidential. Anyone applying will undergo full investigation to determine sanity."[1] Wow!

Is that the way it works?

Is the church really supposed to be managed by a few superpersons trying to meet expectations far beyond reality? What is the Lord's plan for organization, management, and church life in general?

The Corinthian connection

The Corinthian church is a classic example of a highly talented congregation with unrealistic expectations and confused priorities (1 Cor. 1:7). In its enthusiasm and zeal without adequate knowledge, it became mired in partisan preferences (1 Cor. 1:18-29) and personality cults (1 Cor.1:10-17; 3:1-8).

Reflecting pre-Christian practices, the members went overboard on the design of the church's worship services (1 Cor.14), became self serving in attitude (1 Cor. 11:17-22), allowed unconsecrated leaders freely to practice heinous sins (1 Cor. 5:1, 2), and others to continue sexual misadventures (1 Cor. 6:12-20).

Ethical standards suffered. Lawsuits ensued (1 Cor. 6). Church discipline declined. Misunderstandings of marital relations developed (1 Cor. 7), social inequities arose that denied the teachings of the gospel (1 Cor.8), and doctrinal confusion regarding the resurrection undermined the very basis of apostolic teachings and the foundation of the Christian religion itself (1 Cor.15). The turmoil opened the door to sinister invaders bent on twisting the gospel and the using the church for their own ends (2 Cor.11:1-15).

Maybe Corinth is not so far away after all. As one writer remarks:

> The troubles in Corinth were not essentially different from troubles which plague many of our churches today and Paul's frank discussions of what was going on ring a strikingly contemporary note. He tells it like it is.[2]

The gospel antidote

Understanding and applying the gospel, Paul reminds the Corinthians, is the antidote for this situation. The gospel spawns more than modified behavior; it produces a new creation (2 Cor. 5:17). The newly created individual is assigned an ambassadorship (2 Cor. 20), making each a "living letter" (2 Cor. 3:2). The combined product, the church congregation, lacks no spiritual gift (1 Cor. 1:7) and lives in agreement "one with another" (1 Cor. 1:10). No matter who or what people were prior to the new birth experience, they are now "God's temple" (1 Cor. 3:16). They acquire from Jesus previously unknown wisdom (1 Cor. 2:7), the ability to make sound judgments (1 Cor. 2:15; 6:1, 2), and the competence to use freedom in Christ judiciously (1 Cor. 10:23, 24). The goal of the individual member and the church as a congregation is to "do all for the glory of God" (1 Cor. 10:31), a perspective that motivates church members to "seek the good of the many, that they may be saved" (1 Cor. 10:33).

Spiritual gifts: the unifying force

The unifying force to accomplish this in the church congregation is the application of spiritual gifts (1 Cor. 12:7). The process works like the human anatomical system. Every part depends on another. The systematic application of individual spiritual gifts unites the church congregation around a common goal (1 Cor. 12:25), and the gospel "trumpet" can then give a "clear call to battle" (1 Cor. 14:8).

Biblical perspectives on spiritual gifts

Scripture doesn't define exactly what a spiritual gift is. It names many gifts, describes their role in the overall organizational pattern of the church, and illustrates them in action.

Many definitions of gifts have been cited: a channel through which the Holy Spirit ministers to the church, supernatural gifts of grace given as a stewardship to members, abilities to function in a particular service, divine endowments, unique capacities, and special attributes. In this book we will use as a working definition: "A spiritual gift is a special attribute given by the Holy Spirit to every member of the body of Christ, according to God's grace, for use within the context of the body."[3]

First Peter 4:7-11 gives an overview of how spiritual gifts function. As part of a discussion of the Christian lifestyle, Peter employs the phrase "each one should use whatever gift he has received to serve others, faithfully administering God's grace in its various forms" (1 Peter 4:10). "God's grace" in this verse is identified as having "various forms." In verses 7-11, these forms are associated with hospitality and serving, identified in other texts as spiritual gifts. "Faithful administration" indicates that the Lord expects dedicated discipleship in the use of spiritual gifts.

In this passage Peter enunciates five principles about spiritual gifts:

1. An awareness of the urgency of the times in which we live should cause us to give priority to the exercise of our gifts (vs. 7).
2. We will be held accountable for the use of our spiritual gifts (vs. 10).
3. Gifts should be used authoritatively, because we know they are from God (vs. 11).
4. The use of spiritual gifts should bring glory to God, not ourselves (vs. 11).
5. God should always get the credit for the use of spiritual gifts, whether they are supportive gifts or high-profile leadership gifts (vs. 11).

Ellen White makes five significant points regarding the phrase "the manifold grace of God":

A. "None need mourn that they cannot glorify God by talents He never gave them and for which they are not responsible."

2. "God requires no more of them than to improve upon what they have, as stewards of His grace."

3. "The varied trusts are proportioned to our varied capabilities."

4. "Heaven apportions to all their work, and it should be their ambition to do this work well, according to their capabilities."

5. "God requires that all, the weakest as well as the strongest, fulfill their appointed work."—*Testimonies*, 2:245.

The call to discipleship

The use of spiritual gifts is part of the larger picture of Christian *discipleship*—a modern term for Christian service. It implies that active service on behalf of the Kingdom is an integral part of the new-birth experience. Being born again is more than a personal experience. It turns one into a Christian soldier, ready to fight on behalf of the Kingdom of God. Ellen White states: "Every true disciple is born into the Kingdom of God as a missionary."— *The Desire of Ages*, 195. A disciple is a person who has been born again, joined the church, identified his or her spiritual gifts, accepted a role in the church compatible with those gifts, and is committed to fulfilling that role *without continual external motivation*. This definition is based on the Great Commission in Matt. 28:18-20:

> Then Jesus came to them and said, "All authority in heaven and on earth has been given to me. Therefore go and make disciples of all nations, baptizing them in the name of the Father and of the Son and of the Holy Spirit, and teaching them to obey everything I have commanded you. And surely I am with you always, to the very end of the age."

The key elements in this passage are:

- A statement of Jesus' authority
- The command to "Go"
- The ultimate outcome: "Make disciples"

- The communication of truth: "Teach"
- The visible testimony: "Baptize"

The Greek original demonstrates that "going," "teaching," and "baptizing" are part of a simultaneous process of "making disciples"—a circle, not a time line.[4] Church plans should be designed in ways that bring these elements into play simultaneously. The application of spiritual gifts throughout the program of the church will do just that. Discipleship, then, involves the application of individual spiritual gifts to the development and practice of ministries that match a person's gifts.

Is this really important?

I know what you're thinking—I've been sitting in the church for years, and I've heard much about this business of spiritual gifts before. Now you're telling me that these gifts are the framework around which I am supposed to build a ministry? Is this really all that important?

Paul thinks so: "Now about spiritual gifts, brothers, I do not want you to be ignorant" (1 Cor. 12:1). If you don't know what your gifts are, they can't be put to use effectively or intentionally. If you recognize your gifts, you can take steps to develop them to maximum efficiency and usefulness and set priorities for your service to the Kingdom. You will be much more satisfied and less frustrated knowing that you are doing exactly what the Lord has called you to do on behalf of the Kingdom. You will know you are contributing to the overall work of the body of Christ in precisely the way you were meant to contribute.

Gifts and talents

Aren't spiritual gifts merely amplifications or applications of natural talents and abilities? According to Paul, spiritual gifts are assigned by the Holy Spirit to be employed within the context of advancing the Kingdom of God (1 Cor. 12:11). The Spirit may decide to amplify a natural talent and give it a twist that makes it applicable to the advancement of the

Kingdom. He may, on the other hand, decide to assign a person a gift that has little or nothing to do with natural talents or abilities.

Ellen White concurs: "The talents that Christ entrusts to His church represent especially the gifts and blessings imparted by the Holy Spirit."—*Christ's Object Lessons*, 327.

A biblical illustration is the case of Bezalel and the construction team of the desert tabernacle. Bezalel and his assistant, Oholiab, were given "skill, ability and knowledge in all kinds of crafts" by the Holy Spirit (Exod. 35:31). These skill are not mentioned in the New Testament as spiritual gifts. Notice, however, that they also received "the ability to teach others" (vs. 34), and "skill and ability to know how to carry out all the work" (Exod. 36:1). These correspond to the spiritual gifts of teaching and administration mentioned in the New Testament.

Gifts and tasks

"Oh, good. Now that I know I have the gift of teaching, I don't have to show up any more to church work bees. That's for people with gifts of construction, or whatever."

Sorry, it doesn't work that way!

"My church has so few members that we all have to do everything. If we only employ our identifiable gifts, a lot of things won't get done."

There's a solution to this problem as well. Spiritual gifts are assignments of a life-long, primary ministry or ministries. That doesn't preclude fulfilling tasks that have to be done. The difference is that tasks are short-term and based on current needs. Ministries based on spiritual giftedness are long-term. Spiritual giftedness implies expertise, continuing education and consistent development. A dedicated disciple with the gift of teaching may rake leaves occasionally, but he or she will become really good at teaching.

Mine's better

Not really. There are no better or worse gifts. They are all part of the same package and should all give glory to God.

Apollos, the man with the gift of teaching (Acts 18:24-26) was part of the overall scene, as was Barnabas, who had the gift of encouragement (Acts 11:23). Tabitha's gift of mercy was just as valuable as anyone else's (Acts 9:36).

One writer describes two common abuses of spiritual gifts that destroy their effectiveness: gift exaltation and gift projection.[5] Gift exaltation is the idea that some gifts (especially mine) are better than others. Paul's answer is:

> What, after all, is Apollos? And what is Paul? Only servants, through whom you came to believe—as the Lord has assigned to each his task. I planted the seed, Apollos watered it, but God made it grow. So neither he who plants nor he who waters is anything, but only God, who makes things grow. The man who plants and the man who waters have one purpose, and each will be rewarded according to his own labor. For we are God's fellow workers; you are God's field, God's building. By the grace God has given me, I laid a foundation as an expert builder, and someone else is building on it. But each one should be careful how he builds. For no one can lay any foundation other than the one already laid, which is Jesus Christ."—1 Cor 3:5-9.

Gift projection is the idea that everyone else ought to have my gift. If I'm an evangelist, you should be, too. If I have the gift of administration, how come you're so disorganized? In the parable of the talents, the point wasn't how many talents each person had, but what they did with what they had (Matt. 25:14-29).

One happy family

In 1 Cor. 12, Paul uses the analogy of the cooperative functions of human anatomy as an illustration of how spiritual gifts produce unity within the church body. "Now to each one the Spirit is given for the common good" (vs. 7). Verses 12, 13, and 27 explain that the Holy Spirit designs to keep the church unified through the recognition and application of spiritual gifts. The glue that bonds the unity and makes it effective through right attitudes and personality traits is love (1 Cor. 13).

All spiritual gifts are of equal value, even though some function in the background and some are highly visible. In Rom. 12:3, Paul pulls these concepts together by defining the "sober judgment" that keeps people humble as the "measure of faith" the Holy Spirit gives each Christian. The "measure of faith" is then identified as a believer's set of spiritual gifts.

Our Corinthian contemporaries revisited

Paul responded to the Corinthian problem by explaining the role and function of spiritual gifts.

1 Cor. 12:1-11. The true test of spirituality is submission to Jesus.

1 Cor. 12:12-27. All spiritual gifts are important, and operating together in harmony, each contributes to the whole.

1 Cor. 12:28-31. No single gift is a test of spiritual maturity. They are interdependent and have no hierarchy of value, even though some carry a more visible profile than others.

1 Cor. 13. A proper attitude of love underlying the use of spiritual gifts is the essential ingredient that makes the entire system workable.

1 Cor. 14. The relative value of a spiritual gift is its usefulness within the context of the church as a whole. This point is illustrated by a discussion of the confused and inappropriate worship services in Corinth.

Summary

Disciples are expected to use faithfully their assigned gifts to advance the work of the Kingdom. Paul illustrates the interrelationships of the various gifts by comparing them to the coordinated functioning of the human body. They are given for the benefit of all and serve to unify the testimony of the church. Sometimes gifts enhance natural abilities, and sometimes they are entirely different. It all depends on the endowment given by the Holy Spirit.

Notes:

1. William McRae, *The Dynamics of Spiritual Gifts* (Grand Rapids, Mich.: Zondervan Publishing House, 1976), 123, 124.
2. C. Peter Wagner, *Effective Body Building*: San Bernardino, Calif.: Here's Life Publishers, Inc., 1982), 32.
3. C. Peter Wagner, *Your Spiritual Gifts Can Help Your Church Grow*, revised edition (Ventura, Calif.:.Regal Books, 1994), p. 34.
4. Dennis Oliver, *Make Disciples* (Pasadena, Calif.: Fuller Theological Seminary, Dr. of Miss. Dissertation, 1973).
5. C. Peter Wagner, *Your Spiritual Gifts Can Help Your Church Grow*, revised edition (Ventura, Calif.: Regal Books, 1994), 45-48.

TWO

The Holy Spirit and Spiritual Gifts

The Holy Spirit is the active agent assigned by heaven as the Head of the church on earth today. The Holy Spirit energized and launched the early church (Acts 1:8), gave people the instantaneous ability to speak in languages not their own (Acts 2:4), turned frightened disciples into bold preachers (Acts 4:3), directly indicated certain people for certain missions (Acts 13:2), solved doctrinal problems (Acts 15:28), prohibited missionaries from entering certain areas (Acts 16:6), directed them to other areas (Acts 16:10), and was the power behind all kinds of miracles and extraordinary happenings (Acts 19).

The book of Acts mentions the Holy Spirit fifty-seven times and carefully notes that every major decision of the young church was made under His guidance. The disciples waited for the Holy Spirit before beginning to preach. He fell on each new group of believers: on Jews (4:31), then on Samaritans (8:17), then Gentiles (10:44), and finally on some of John the Baptist's disciples (19:6). The Spirit personally directed each major advance of the church. He sent Philip into the desert to meet the Ethiopian (8:29), set apart missionaries (13:2), guided the first major church council (15:1-8), and helped plan Paul's itinerary (13:4; 16:6).

The *Index to the Writings of Ellen White* has fifty-nine columns on the Holy Spirit. The following list indicates some of the ways the Holy Spirit is active in the church and in the lives of individual members:

1. Gives mental power (6T, 306).
2. Gives healing power (MYP, 30).
3. Renews motives and affections (AA, 284).
4. Gives the ability to accomplish good works (MB, 80).
5. Gives supernatural strength (GW, 286).
6. Brings unity to the church (5T, 227).
7. Gives us training that fits us for heaven (7T, 273).

The Holy Spirit and spiritual gifts

Spiritual gifts are intimately connected with the appearance of the Holy Spirit. From the day of Pentecost onward, the Holy Spirit becomes the administrator of the Christian church and the assigner of spiritual gifts, tools used for the advancement of the kingdom.

Paul refers to spiritual gifts as "spiritualities," the appointed activities of spiritual persons—that is, born again Christians. He uses two Greek words: *pneumatikos*, which means "spirituals," and *charisma*, which means "gift." *Pneumatikos*, an adjective, appears only after the day of Pentecost in connection with people filled, moved, and governed by the Spirit of God. It has its roots in the word *pnuema*, Greek for "spirit," the essential or vital force that energizes a living being.

The baptism of the Holy Spirit

The Bible talks about three kinds of baptism: water baptism, the baptism of the Holy Spirit, and the baptism of fire:

> I baptize you with water for repentance. But after me will come one who is more powerful than I, whose sandals I am not fit to carry. He will baptize you with the Holy Spirit and with fire (Matthew 3:11).

The baptism of the Holy Spirit is an empowerment for service. It is what makes the mission enterprise of the church function effectively. It works on the converted mind and heart, building in new concepts and a new vision. Notice a significant statement from Ellen White:

> The Spirit of God, as it comes into the heart by faith, is the beginning of the life eternal. With the baptism of the Holy Spirit upon the teacher of truth, he can talk of Christ and him crucified in language that savors of heaven. The mind and spirit of Christ will be in him, and he can present the will of God to man because his own heart has been brought into submission, and has been glorified by the Spirit of God. The Sun of Righteousness is risen upon him, that he might reflect its brightness to the world, and he will give evidence in a holy life that the truth he has received has been a sanctifying principle, and not a mere theory.[1]

The key Bible text about the baptism of the Holy Spirit is Acts 1:8: "But you will receive power when the Holy Spirit comes on you, and you will be my witnesses." Two experiences in the Bible point out how this happened. The first is the experience on the Day of Pentecost. In the Upper Room, Peter got the idea of reorganizing the church along Old Testament lines (Acts 1:15-26). Those present used an Old Testament system of casting lots and chose Matthias. Then, as Acts 2:2 points out, the Holy Spirit arrived "suddenly." It empowered them instantaneously (Acts 2:4). Peter's reorganization scheme disappears, along with Matthias. All of a sudden, the disciples are out on the street preaching and making converts. That is the baptism of the Holy Spirit.[2]

The second experience took place in the city of Ephesus (Acts 19). Paul discovered some disciples of John the Baptist in the city who knew nothing about the Holy Spirit. Once they understood, and the power arrived, they were out on the streets witnessing. As a result, the city and the surrounding provinces learned about Christianity. Empowerment for service—that's the key.

Baptism of fire

The Bible mentions a baptism of fire only once, in Matt. 3:11, quoted above. There are a number of views as to what this baptism means.[3] Some believe it is synonymous with water baptism in the sense that water and fire are both symbols of purification.[4] Others believe it is a reference to the tongues of fire on the Day of Pentecost. Yet others see it as a third work of grace evidenced by speaking in tongues and entire sanctification.[5]

Ellen White connects this baptism with the prophecy of the golden bowls and the oil in Zech. 4. The oil represents the Holy Spirit, the golden bowls the hearts of the messengers who are both empowered and given zeal to preach the message:

> These empty themselves into the golden bowls, which represent the hearts of the living messengers of God, who bear the Word of the Lord to the people in warnings and entreaties. The Word itself must be as represented, the golden oil, emptied from the two olive trees that stand by the Lord of the whole earth. This is the baptism by the Holy Spirit with fire. This will open the soul of unbelievers to conviction. The wants of the soul can be met only by the working of the Holy Spirit of God. Man can of himself do nothing to satisfy the longings and meet the aspirations of the heart.[6]

Her view is supported by a statement by Paul in 1 Thess. 5:19; "Do not put out the Spirit's fire." The "Spirit's fire" is equated with the gifts of prophecy and discernment, adding credibility to the fire as the content of the message combined with the zeal of the messenger. The three baptisms are really three facets of one event. Water baptism is a personal testimony in a public forum to the renewal, regeneration, and new birth that have taken place in a person's life. The baptism of the Holy Spirit empowers for service. On a personal level, the baptism of fire adds zeal and daring to a person's witness. On a congregational level, the baptism of fire revives dreary church services and converts then into dynamic soul-winning and soul-sustaining tools of the Spirit.

The Holy Spirit: church administrator

The book of Acts portrays the Holy Spirit as a presiding presence in the early church. He was in command. In many situations, He directly indicated what the church should do. Paul referred to this aspect of the Holy Spirit's work when he told Timothy not to neglect his gift, given him "though a prophetic message when the body of elders laid their hands on you" (1 Tim. 4:14).

In Acts 13:2-4, the Holy Spirit directly names Paul and Barnabas as missionaries and empowers them for the task through the laying on of hands. The Holy Spirit worked through the church, and the church recognized the voice of the Spirit. The decision of the Jerusalem council regarding the role of Gentiles in the church was approved, James says, "by the Holy Spirit and us," implying a close connection and communication system between the church and the Holy Spirit (Acts 15:28). In two cases, the Holy Spirit kept Paul and his companions from going to certain areas—and then through a dream directing them to a different place (Acts 16:6-10).

The Holy Spirit also directed individual lives during the era of the early church. Jesus' words: "But you know him, for he lives with you and will be in you" (John 14:17) came true. The experience of the twelve followers of John the Baptist living in Ephesus is a case in point (Acts 19:1-7). They knew nothing about the Holy Spirit, but once they learned about Him, their lives changed dramatically.

The Holy Spirit: source of power

Jesus promised the disciples power (Acts 1:8). It arrived on the day of Pentecost in the person of the Holy Spirit. Only with this power could a handful of people accomplish the task of preaching the gospel throughout the world. Paul reminds us that the gospel is the "power" of God unto salvation (Rom. 1:16). The gospel is not an undercover operation. It ought to be out on the street and shouting its message from the housetops. By power, we mean something that is active. It works. Passive, inactive Christians do not have power. People who have only an intellectual attachment to Christianity do not have power. Born again but undiscipled Christians do not have power.[7] The Holy Spirit takes the power of the gospel and turns it into dynamic Christian activism.

There are a number of Greek words for power. One is *kratos*, which implies physical strength. Another, *exousia*, implies the authority given a ruler. Jesus used this word when he said, "All power is given unto me in heaven and in earth." The word used in Acts 1:8—"you shall receive power"—however, is *dunamis*, a word that implies explosive energy.

The Greek translation of the Hebrew Scriptures uses *dunamis* six times in Ps. 68:28-35. The Old Testament Israelite worshipers pleaded for God to show and use His power. On the day of Pentecost it arrived in a new and dynamic way. Suddenly, the disciples were "gifted" by the Holy Spirit to do what they could not do under normal circumstances. The church today draws on that same power source for personal Christian experience and to expand its mission of taking the gospel to whomever has not yet heard it.

One of the most evident areas of the Holy Spirit's working is in the realm of the power or sign gifts such as prophecy, healing, deliverance, and miracles. To understand the power of the Holy Spirit in these areas, we need to understand Satan's organizational system.

Paul frequently talks about "the powers." The key text is Eph. 6:12: "For our struggle is not against flesh and blood, but against rulers, against authorities, against the powers of this dark world and against the spiritual forces of evil in the heavenly realms." These spiritual forces of evil are "world rulers" who "blind the minds of unbelievers" (2 Cor. 4:4). The world is in the grip of these powers. Except for the angels, who do the will of God (Gal. 3:19), these powers are in opposition to God. A gigantic cosmic host of evil powers is holding humankind enslaved. The entire complex of the "spirit of the world" (1 Cor. 2:12) is in this grip. These powers manifest themselves in various ways, often unseen and inexplicable.

God is still ultimately in control (Rom. 1:21), but the powers are nevertheless sinister influences in the world. They exercise a great deal of influence over the course of the present age.

In Paul's view, this complex of powers is a highly organized system led by Satan and administered by his evil angels. Whatever happens in the world outside of Christ is influenced by them. They do not, however, have complete control. John affirms that there are good angels holding back the winds of strife until the Lord decides it is time to wind down the great controversy (Rev. 7, 16). Paul makes the point that in spite of the complex structure the powers have in place, Jesus "disarmed the powers and authorities and made a public spectacle of them, triumphing over them by the cross." (Col. 2:15). The powers fight a lost cause, but don't underestimate the power of Satan. He is not about to give up without combat.

How Satan ties up humanity

To understand this issue, we must first understand how Satan ties up the human race. He does four things:

1. He blinds people's spiritual eyes. 2 Cor. 4:4,
2. He blocks spiritual discernment. 1 Cor. 2:14.
3. He causes people to see evil as good and thus negates the power of the gospel. Rom. 1:24.
4. He distorts spiritual discernment with false doctrine. Rev. 14:8.

Power for effective evangelism

The power for effective evangelism, the means of undoing what Satan has done, comes only from the Holy Spirit. Please notice that it is power for *effective* evangelism that comes from the Holy Spirit. It is possible to do a lot of churchy things without the power of the Holy Spirit. You can win souls without the power of the Holy Spirit by convincing people through logic. You can inundate people with biblical data. You can even talk people to death to the point that they may join the church just to get rid of you. None of this, however, constitutes *effective* evangelism.

Effective evangelism only happens when the Holy Spirit is allowed to work in such a way that three things transpire:

1. People's minds are unchained from the power of Satan.
2. Their spiritual eyes are enlightened.
3. The power of the gospel takes effect in their lives.

No logic, power of persuasion, evangelistic technology, or power of personality can pull this off. None of these things can occur without the aid and influence of the Holy Spirit.

People's minds are unchained when the gospel is presented with power. That doesn't mean with a large amplifier and a "loud cry." It means through a dynamic personal testimony that rings true. It means saying what you say about the Lord with conviction in your voice and enthusiasm in your body language. It means beating the blahs in your own life and getting out and beating the bushes for converts, because unless you and I do it, someone is going to miss heaven.

What does all this have to do with spiritual gifts? The Holy Spirit both empowers and equips church members for ministry. That ministry takes on the kingdom of Satan by living the gospel, which in itself is power, proclaiming in many and varied ways what the gospel has done and can do and persuading people to enter the kingdom of God. The entire panoply of spiritual gifts is geared toward this objective, and the kingdom of God prospers when they are used effectively.

The Holy Spirit: teacher

Besides being church administrator and the source of power, the Holy Spirit is also the church's principle teacher. "The Counselor, the Holy Spirit, whom the Father shall send in my name, *will teach you* all things and *will remind you* of everything I have said to you." (John 14:26). Ellen White reminds us: "Jesus has perpetuated His earthly teaching ministry through the Spirit."[8] This teaching office is as dynamic as was the experience of Pentecost. "God can teach you more in one moment by His Holy Spirit than you could learn from the great men of the earth."[9]

The Holy Spirit as teacher (1) brings out new insights, (2)

instructs in "what is yet to come," (3) brings glory to God by helping us understand more fully and completely, and (4) draws from God's fountain of knowledge and teaches it to us. He teaches in two principle ways: by illuminating our minds as we study the Scriptures, and through the gift of teaching given to certain church members whose ministry is to teach well (2 Tim. 2:1, 2).

The Holy Spirit: assigner of gifts

People have many ideas about how a person receives or is assigned a spiritual gift. Some believe that the church decides who gets which gifts. Others feel that election to church office is the same as receiving a particular gift. Some people believe that only their pastor has any spiritual gifts, and that church members are supposed to just listen and do whatever he or she says. Others believe that anyone can do anything and that no one has any authority over another.

The Holy Spirit assigns gifts to people according to His sovereign will: "All these are the work of one and the same Spirit, and he gives them to each one, just as he determines" (1 Cor. 12:11).

We are all responsible for turning our individual gifts into ministries that will advance the work of the Kingdom. Paul says he was "appointed" to his ministry with a specific target audience in mind, non-Jews (Acts 9:15; 2 Tim. 2:7). This ministry corresponds to the spiritual gifts chosen for Paul by the Holy Spirit.

The assignment of gifts by the Holy Spirit is designed to advance the Lord's work. The church is set up as a corporate body to do the work of the Kingdom by organizing the gifts of the members into effective ministries. In this sense, the church has the authority of the Holy Spirit to administer the collective gifts of the members.

The Holy Spirit and intercessory prayer

The arrival of the Holy Spirit at Pentecost was no accident. The Lord planned to unveil Him in a new way at that moment in history, because the time was opportune. More than a million people from all over the known world were in the city for the festival. Many were receptive to the gospel.

Without the right kind of people to do the job, however, the outpouring of the Holy Spirit could not have happened. The Holy Spirit *enables and equips* people to do a job, He doesn't usually do the job Himself. It is through intercessory prayer that the Holy Spirit responds to the call of the church, or individuals, for that empowerment (James 1:5; 4:13-18).

Intercessory prayer is a special kind of prayer. It requests specific things from the Lord, based on what He has promised. The Lord does not withhold what He has promised, but He does not always confer it unless we ask for it.

There are seven levels of prevailing intercessory prayer:

Level 1: Ask (Matt. 7:7).
Level 2: Seek (Matt. 7:7).
Level 3: Knock (Matt. 7:7).
Level 4: Fast (Ps. 35:13).
Level 5: Prayer burden for a specific thing (Neh. 2:2-5).
Level 6: Wrestling in prayer (Luke 22:44; Col. 4:12; Gen. 32:22-30).
Level 7: Prayer warfare. Specific battles with Satan (Matt. 4:1-11).

Any combination of levels may be involved when praying for a specific issue. The Lord honors these prayers and the Holy Spirit goes into action on our behalf.

Summary:

The Holy Spirit is the active agent, assigned by God the Father, to be the administrator of the church on earth. For both the church body and individual Christians, He is the source of power and the primary teacher, illuminating minds and leading to truth. He assigns spiritual gifts, both to individual members and to the church as a body. Intercessory prayer, based on claiming the promises of God, is the effective instrument the church should use to activate the Holy Spirit on its behalf.

Notes:

1. *Bible Echo and Signs of the Times*, March 1, 1892.
2. For a training course on how his can happen in your church, see Garrie F. Williams, *How to Be Filled With the Holy Spirit and Know It* (Hagerstown, Md.: Review and Herald Publishing Association, 1991).
3. The *Seventh-day Adventist Bible Commentary* cites a number of views but takes no position (5:300).
4. LeRoy E. Froom, *The Coming of the Comforter* (Washington, D.C.: Review and Herald Publishing Association, 1931), 269.
5. See Stanley M. Burgess and Gary B. McGee (eds.) "Fire-Baptized Holiness Church," *Dictionary of Pentecostal and Charismatic Movements* (Grand Rapids, Mich.: Zondervan Publishing House, 1988), 309.
6. MS 109, 1897 (*Seventh-day Adventist Bible Commentary*), 4:1180.
7. It seems strange that there could be such a person. Look up Luke 15:25-31 to read about one of them.
8. Ellen G. White, *Sons and Daughters of God*, 282.
9. White, *Testimonies to Ministers*, 119.

THREE

Spiritual Gifts and the Church

All churches have to organize themselves in some way. In 1957, *Ministry* magazine published the organizational systems of a number of churches. One diagram of a major metropolitan Seventh-day Adventist church is magnificent. It's a wheel with the membership as the hub, and spokes radiating through the boards of elders and deacons—each with its subcommittees—to eight major committees dealing with all kinds of church activities.[1] Another church had nineteen committees, seven projects underway, and six unfinished projects under study. One author wrote, regarding the annual election process:

> When we find, as we do in too many instances, that the wrong persons are elected to good offices where they either (in many cases) do nothing or (in a few cases) do wrong, the reason probably lies in the way in which nominations and elections are handled.[2]

His solution was to select the best possible person as chairperson of the nominating committee, and for the pastor to provide careful guidance over the electoral process. Things haven't changed much since 1957. The same general patterns of organization can be found today. Staffing all the committees is still a major problem, and the advice about nominating committees is about the same.

None of these organizational plans, systems, or outlines, however, mention anything about spiritual gifts and their role in the church. How can spiritual gifts help a church meet its organizational needs? In search of an answer, let's take a look at two organizational patterns illustrated in the Bible.

The Jethro system (Exodus 18)

This system came about when an overworked Moses tried to do everything himself. It was a good management technique designed to solve an organizational problem. Jethro simply split Moses' various tasks into small units and delegated responsibility to more people. The large tasks are often called "macro" management, the smaller, more detailed ones, "micro" management. The Jethro system allows for efficiency in both macro and micro management. Ellen White comments:

> The time and strength of those who in the providence of God have been placed in leading positions of responsibility in the church should be spent in dealing with the weightier matters demanding special wisdom and largeness of heart. It is not in the order of God that such men should be appealed to for the adjustment of minor matters that others are well qualified to handle.[3]

Ezekiel saw the wheels

Another organizational pattern was revealed to Ezekiel while he pastored a local congregation of exiles in Kebar, Babylon. The Lord showed him a system of intricately intertwined living beings, wheels, and wings, sustained and operated by the Holy Spirit.

> When the living creatures moved, the wheels beside them moved; and when the living creatures rose from the ground, the wheels also rose. Wherever the spirit would go, they would go, and the wheels would rise along with them, because the

> spirit of the living creatures was in the wheels (Eze. 1:19, 20).

In this system, the Lord's Spirit directs the motion of the "wheels" so that they produce coordinated action, beautiful exactness and perfect harmony.[4]

Comparing the two systems

The Jethro system is excellent for organizing major tasks into small units and involving a lot of people to get the job done. It also functions especially well when there is a clear "chain of command" from top to bottom.

The Ezekiel system functions well when many seemingly unrelated tasks need to be done and a central core of unity is necessary to accomplish those tasks.

Both systems are useful in the church. The Ezekiel system, however, identifies closely with the nature of the local church. A local church is made up of a group of people who hold common beliefs but must do varied, equally important, tasks to keep both the internal and outreach programs of the church intact.

This is where spiritual gifts come in. When the people in the seemingly diverse group called a congregation function in the particular ministry area assigned them by the Lord through their spiritual gifts, they not only function effectively, but happily. They recognize they are fulfilling the call of the Lord, and they feel fulfilled, energized, and competent. Designing the church organizational system around spiritual giftedness avoids the problem cited by the author above of having the wrong persons elected to good offices, with the consequence that in many cases they either do nothing or, in a few cases, do wrong.

The ministry of all believers

Peter describes the church as a "royal priesthood" (1 Pet. 2:9, 10). The *priesthood* of all believers emphasized by the Reformers focused on the fact that all Christians can go directly to God in prayer. They need no intermediary priest to have access to God. The *ministry* of all believers focuses on the fact that all believers are called to ministry. It is not just the paid clergy who are responsible for the destiny of the church and its members.

The ministry of all believers is more commonly called *discipleship* today. All Christians are called to discipleship. As Ellen White puts it, "If we are Christians, this work will be our delight. No sooner is one converted than there is born within him a desire to make known to others what a precious friend he has found in Jesus."[5]

The New Testament *ekklesia*

Congregational life today usually centers on church buildings. In New Testament times, believers met in home churches (Rom. 16:5; 1 Cor. 16:19; Col. 4:15) for worship and fellowship (Acts 2:24-47). There was no particular organizational model behind this system—the people simply needed some place to meet. There was, however, a bond between the members, embodied in the use of the Greek word *ekklesia*. This word embraces the meaning of a group of "called out" persons bound together by common beliefs and a spiritual unity: "For we were all baptized by one Spirit into one body—and we were all given the one Spirit to drink" (1 Cor. 12:13).

This *ekklesia* was the creation of God through the Holy Spirit, formed on the day of Pentecost by unifying the languages of the audience through a miraculous intervention. It began with a reversal of the language confusion at the Tower of Babel and resulted in a universal fellowship bound together by common beliefs, discipleship, respect, and love.

Early church leadership

The leadership core in the early church was built around the original apostles and the assignment of spiritual gifts by the Holy Spirit. Spiritual giftedness had a high profile in the early church. Historian Lars Qualben writes,

> The early church organization was not centered in office and in law [i.e. canon law or policies], but in the special gifts of the Spirit. An elder might also teach, preach, and administer the Sacraments, but

> he did not do so because he was an elder, but because he had the 'gift.'[6]

The apostles and other spiritually gifted people spoke with an authority derived from God Himself, not from election to office.[7] The Holy Spirit chose some additional apostles (Acts 13:1-3; Gal. 2:6-9).[8] Other leaders were chosen because of a specific need in the church (Acts 6) and were assigned particular spiritual gifts (Acts 6:8-10; 9:10).[9] These people were often identified as *pneumatikos*, meaning persons gifted by the Holy Spirit—for example, prophets (Acts 11:27, 28; 13:1; 21:10) and teachers (Acts 13:1).

The food distribution problem in Acts 6 gave birth to the office of deacon. The Scripture also specifically mentions the spiritual giftedness of these deacons. The office of elder came into being (Acts 11:30), though the Bible says nothing about how or when they were first chosen and named. By the time of the Jerusalem council, some fourteen years after the stoning of Stephen, elders and apostles were recognized as sharing the leadership of the church (Acts 15:6).

Paul was both an apostle and a spiritually gifted disciple. He began his ministry to the Gentiles because he was called to do so by the Lord "from birth" (Acts 9:15; 1 Tim. 2:16; Eph. 3:8; Gal. 1:15) and was subsequently commanded to do so (Acts 13:47) and "entrusted with this task" (Rom. 11:13; Gal. 2:7). He was given a special gift (Eph. 3:8), and carrying out his ministry became his "priestly duty" (Rom. 15:16). His call to this ministry was affirmed through Ananias at the time of his conversion (Acts 9:15), reaffirmed by the Holy Spirit at the time of his dedication to mission service (Acts 13:1-3), and confirmed again by Peter at the Jerusalem council (Acts 15:7; Gal. 2:6-10).

Making decisions in the early church

How did the early Christian church make major decisions? A clue is found in the resolution of the issues dealt with at the Jerusalem council in Acts 15. The "apostles and elders" met to consider the circumcision issue (15:6). Paul says he went to the meeting in "response to a revelation" (Gal. 2:2)—an indication of his prophetic gift. There was "much discussion," and finally Peter, recognized as a primary authority, related his experience with Cornelius (Acts 10), which involved both a direct revelation from God and the application of one of the "power" gifts (Acts 10). Paul and Barnabas then told their stories.

The astonished assembly "became silent as they listened" (vs. 12). James, the council chairperson, made a "judgment," supported by Old Testament evidence, that the gospel would go to the Gentiles (vss. 15-21). His decision is stated in the minutes of the meeting as having "seemed good to the Holy Spirit and to us" (vs. 28). The apostles, elders "and the whole church" approved of the final letter and the messengers who delivered it (vs. 22).

The early church made decisions based on instruction from the Scriptures, the direct guidance of the Holy Spirit, and the accumulative counsel of the membership. Paul used this model, including the utilization of spiritual gifts, as a design for the unified functioning of the church (Rom. 12; 1 Cor. 12; Eph. 4).

This system, including the utilization of spiritual gifts, interfaces with the Ezekiel model:

> The striking feature of divine operations is the accomplishment of the greatest work that can be done in our world by very simple means. It is God's plan that every part of His government shall depend on every other part, the whole as a wheel within a wheel, working with entire harmony. He moves upon human forces, causing His Spirit to touch invisible chords, and the vibration rings to the extremity of the universe.[10]

Who has the authority?

The question naturally arises of who has the authority to do what in the church? Whenever this issue came up in the New Testament church, the answers focused on the primacy of the mission of the church and the unity needed to fulfill its mission. The church was not authorized to preach "another gospel" (Gal. 1:6, 7). The original deacons were named so that the apostles would not be obliged to "neglect the ministry of the word of God" (Acts 6:2). The church should be "perfectly united in mind and thought" (1 Cor. 1:10) for the glory of God (1 Cor. 10:31) and the common good of the membership (1 Cor. 12:7).

People who wouldn't recognize the moral stipulations that are part of the gospel were expelled (1 Cor. 5:12), lawsuits using outside courts were out of place because the saints are capable of "judging angels" (1 Cor. 6:3). Everything is permissible, but not everything is beneficial (1 Cor. 6:12), meaning that people ought to exercise "sober judgment" and keep their personal pride in check (Rom 12:3). The time has thus come to "wake up from slumber" and get the job done (Rom. 13:11).

How does this apply to us?

The primary leadership selection process in the Seventh-day Adventist church is through a representative electoral process. It is an international body led by democratically elected officials who serve for designated periods of time and may or may not be continued in office. Two sets of elected local church officers, elders and deacons/deaconesses, are installed through a special ceremony of laying on of hands. The laying on of hands is done by those previously installed as elders, and is a lifelong commissioning, though applicable only if elected by the local congregation. In a sense, the democratic features of the system override the laying on of hands endowment.

Where do spiritual gifts fit?

We are used to organizing church life around standard needs: looking after the church building, visiting members who are ill, designing worship services, etc. The usual pattern is to list the jobs to be done and then find some people willing and available to do them, or who have built up a certain seniority that seems to make them automatically eligible to function. Often the leadership selection process in contemporary churches is based on election due to availability or seniority.

A better way to go is to recognize the close connection between the assignment of spiritual gifts and the assignment to offices or ministries. Paul and Barnabas were first called directly by the Holy Spirit through the prophetic office (Acts 13:1-3) and given the gift of missionary, among others. But the decision was confirmed by the body of the church (Acts 13:3). Timothy's experience was the same. He was called through a prophetic message, and confirmed by the body of the church (1 Tim. 4:14). Adding spiritual giftedness to the electoral process brings in a new dimension to fulfilling the requirements of church organization. It adds strength and discipleship to what may otherwise be an office in name only rather than a vital part of the advancement of the kingdom.

Illustrations of spiritual giftedness in action

The gift of missionary, for example, involves the ability to use other spiritual gifts in a multi-cultural context (Acts 22:21). Paul's missionary gift was a bridge that made possible the completion of the mandate in Acts 1:8.

The gift of prophecy

Another example is recognition of the gift of prophecy as a lifelong ministry given to Ellen White. This belief is based on Scriptural evidence and the fruits of a lifetime of ministry. The presence of this gift in the church is of inestimable value for developing ministry and for solid counsel. It represents an authoritative voice pointing the church in the right direction, as did the gift of prophecy in the New Testament church.

Summary

The presence of spiritual giftedness in the church needs to be taken into account in the organizational system used to accomplish the mission of the church. The last three chapters of this book outline ways and means of using spiritual gifts in the church.

Notes:

1. "Organizational Chart of the White Memorial Seventh-day Adventist Church," *Ministry*, October, 1957, 29.
2. Leif Kr. Tobiassen, "Adventist Concepts of Church Management," *Ministry*, October, 1957, 35-37.
3. Ellen G. White, *The Acts of the Apostles*, 93.
4. White, *Testimonies for the Church*, 5:751.
5. White, *The Desire of Ages*, 141.
6. Lars Qualben, *A History of the Christian Church* (New York: Thomas Nelson and Sons, 1942), 94.
7. Peter's system for electing new apostles didn't fare well (Acts 1: 15-26). Matthias is never heard of again. The sudden appearance of the Holy Spirit and the manifestation of miraculous spiritual gifts changed Peter's thinking about church organization (1 Pet. 4:10).
8. James, the Lord's brother (Gal. 1:19), Andronicus, and Junias (Rom. 16:7) are also recognized as apostles.
9. For an introduction to this topic, see George Elden Ladd, *A Theology of the New Testament* (Grand Rapids: William B. Eerdmans Publishing Company, 1974), 342-356.
10. White, *Evangelism*, 93.

FOUR

Spiritual Gifts in History

From its inception, the Seventh-day Adventist Church has accepted the view that spiritual gifts are functional in any age. Most Adventist writings on this point focus on the manifestation of the gift of prophecy in the life and ministry of Ellen White. Secondarily, they defend the position that all spiritual gifts are still functional and valid. *Fundamental Belief No. 16*, adopted in 1980, includes all the spiritual gifts as applicable to the life of the church in our contemporary world.

The perpetuity of spiritual gifts

Before considering the history of spiritual gifts, we need to take a look at a view called cessationism. Cessationism is the idea that some general spiritual gifts, such as helps and hospitality, still function, but that gifts which fall into the category of power or sign gifts, such as prophecy and miracles, no longer function. Authority gifts such as the gift of apostleship have also ceased, according to this view.

The cessationist argument declares that the signs, wonders, and miracles of New Testament times were different from miracles today.[1] Cessationist John MacArthur divides the gifts mentioned in Eph. 4 into three categories: gifted people, permanent edifying gifts, and temporary sign gifts. The sign gifts, he maintains, gave the apostles credibility. When the apostles died, the sign gifts ceased.[2] The underlying concept is that once the canon of Scripture was closed, there could be no more revelation. Using the wording of Heb. 2:3 as a chronological anchor point, MacArthur argues that by the time Ephesians and 1 Corinthians were written, the time of miracles was already past. Let's examine this argument.

Heb. 2:3, 4 reads:

> How shall we escape if we ignore such a great salvation? This salvation, which was first announced by the Lord, was confirmed to us by those who heard him. God also testified to it by signs, wonders, and various miracles, and gifts of the Holy Spirit distributed according to his will.

MacArthur's point is that these verses are in the past tense; therefore, they are talking about something that already happened. He argues that because the sign or power gifts are listed in 1 Cor. 12 but not in Rom. 12 or Eph. 4, they had passed from the scene of action. He contends that it was taken for granted by the church that they had ceased. Heb. 2:3, 4 lists a sequence of events: (1) the announcement of salvation by Jesus, (2) affirmation of its veracity by eyewitnesses, and (3) signs and wonders.

The final phrase, "and gifts of the Holy Spirit distributed according to his will" is assumed to mean that these were gifts given to the apostles but not to the church in general. The word translated *gifts* in Heb. 2:4 is *merismos*, which really means to divide or distribute. Seventh-day Adventists see in this distribution a reference to the spiritual gifts mentioned in Romans, Ephesians, and 1 Corinthians. This chronological argument falls apart, however, with a closer look at the dates of the composition of these books. The chronological sequence of books is so close that it is difficult to read so elaborate a cessationist argument just because Paul speaks in the past tense.

Rom. .... A.D. 57-58
1 Cor. .... A.D. 57
Eph. .... A.D. 62
Heb. .... c. A.D. 65

Another line of argument is that the gift lists in various places reflect the purpose of the particular epistle and the situation to which it was addressed. Heb. 2 is part of an affirmation of Jesus as superior to Old Testament angels, Moses, and other traditional Hebrew categories—a view confirmed by eyewitnesses and signs and wonders. It has nothing to do with the continuance or cessation of these signs and wonders.

1 Cor 13:8-13

Another argument used by cessatinists is that 1 Cor. 13:8-13 indicates the passing of these gifts.

What did Paul mean in verse 10 by "when perfection comes, the imperfect disappears"? At what point in history does the perfection he mentions arrive? The word *perfect* in this verse is the Greek word *teleios*, which means "complete when it gets to the end." On this earth, we never attain total "completeness." This only happens at the second coming, when "all things are made new." This is evident from the expression "face to face" in verse 12. This can only refer to the second coming, not a prior point in history.[3]

The Seventh-day Adventist view

The Seventh-day Adventist view begins with the interpretation of Joel 2:28: "And afterward, I will pour out my Spirit on all people. Your sons and daughters will prophesy, your old men will dream dreams, your young men will see visions." Joel 2:28. The Hebrew word for "afterward" in Joel 2:28 means "some time in the future." Peter used the word *escatos* in Greek, which means "last in time or space." The early Christians understood their times to be the last days, because Jesus told them to set up the Kingdom in preparation for His return. That era, however, was not the final "last days."

Adventist pioneer J. N. Andrews took the position that a

denial of the continuance of spiritual gifts automatically denied the work of the Holy Spirit during the Christian era: "Those who reject the work of the Spirit of God under the plea that the Scriptures are sufficient, do deny and reject all that part of the Bible which reveals the office and work of the Holy Spirit."[4] Uriah Smith argued that, based on Joel 2:28, spiritual gifts must cover all the intervening ground between Pentecost and the second coming.[5]

Writing in 1947, L. H. Christian felt that many mainline churches lacked spiritual depth because they did not recognize the importance of spiritual gifts.[6] Carlyle B. Haynes remarked that spiritual gifts are an integral part of the dispensation of the Holy Spirit, the span of time between Pentecost and the second coming.[7] Focusing particularly on the gift of prophecy, long-time General Conference president A.G. Daniells wrote:

> When sin had broken direct communion between heaven and earth, God gave the prophetic gift to men, vouchsafing it to His church, and that gift has never been permanently withdrawn since it was bestowed.[8]

That is an excellent summary, applying equally to all gifts of the Spirit. Ellen White affirms the continuance of spiritual gifts:

> But the gifts of the Spirit are promised to every believer according to his need for the Lord's work. The promise is just as strong and trustworthy now as in the days of the apostles. "These signs shall follow them that believe." This is the privilege of God's children, and faith should lay hold on all that it is possible to have as an indorsement of faith.[9]

Spiritual gifts in church history

Church history does not yield a great deal of information about the appearance and practice of spiritual gifts. There are indications, however, that when some of the more spectacular gifts appeared, they were not perceived as unusual. This in itself is an indication that they were more or less taken for granted as a normal part of Christian life. Ronald A. N. Kydd, who has done a doctoral dissertation on the presence of spiritual gifts in the church up to A.D. 320, has found evidence that the utilization of spiritual gifts was common up until about A.D. 260, after which they faded out.[10] Kydd's conclusion is that after about A.D. 260 spiritual gifts "no longer fitted in the highly organized, well-educated, wealthy, socially-powerful Christian communities."[11] As what we know today as the Roman Catholic Church became established, the bishops took over the functions of the spiritually gifted church members, and eventually, lay persons were shut out of ministry entirely.[12]

Two early church documents, the *Didache* and *The Shepherd of Hermas*, mention ongoing spiritual gifts. Both documents use almost the same words as Paul in listing the various gifts. Justin Martyr, who lived some sixty years after the death of John, the last of the apostles, says: "The prophetical gifts remain with us, even to the present time."[13]

Around A.D. 175, a group called the Montanists claimed to have the sign gifts in their midst. Other writers of the time, even those opposed to Montanism, do not seem to regard the appearance of these spiritual gifts as either inconsistent or impious. Unfortunately, the Montanists took the gift of prophecy to extremes and eventually disappeared.

The appearance of protesting groups such as the Waldenses and Huguenots during the Middle Ages brought a renewed emphasis on spiritual gifts. According to A. G. Daniells, a contemporary observer said of such a group in southeastern France: "They were all people without malice, in whom I perceived nothing that I could suspect of being their invention."[14] Again, unfortunately, many of these groups went to extremes and brought spiritual gifts into disrepute. Usually they emphasized the more spectacular gifts, especially healing, tongues, and prophecy. The unfortunate excesses of such groups led some people such as the famous Spanish mystic,

St. John of the Cross (1542-1591), to denounce all spiritual giftedness as dangerous to a Christian's search for spiritual perfection. St. John of the Cross emphasized personal prayer life as leading to personal holiness, at the expense of public ministry through the application of spiritual gifts.[15] This same perception is not unknown in contemporary Adventism. Our emphasis on personal holiness in preparation for the world to come often unwittingly militates against the development of discipleship and active participation in the advancement of the kingdom.

Renewed interest

Interest in spiritual gifts, especially healing and speaking in tongues, picked up in the early 1880s. Edward Irving in Great Britain sparked a revival with his preaching on the second coming. Unfortunately, he also sparked an enormous controversy when speaking in tongues broke out in his church.[16] Irving accepted the messages given in tongues as superior to biblical authority, a belief that helped give rise to the idea of the secret rapture. There is some evidence that this idea was first mentioned in a revelation by a person influenced by Irving.[17]

In spite of the extremism and unfortunate aberrations, there is enough evidence from church history to show that spiritual gifts have been in existence since New Testament times and did not cease with the time of the apostles.

Spiritual gifts and the latter rain

Adventists have long taught that during the latter rain, signs and wonders will again be manifested in remarkable ways. Ellen White draws a parallel between the early and latter rains:

> The great work of the gospel is not to close with less manifestation of the power of God than marked its opening. The prophecies which were fulfilled in the outpouring of the former rain at the opening of the gospel are again to be fulfilled in the latter rain at its close.[18]

In a further description of the latter rain, she remarks:

> Servants of God, with their faces lighted up and shining with holy consecration, will hasten from place to place to proclaim the message from heaven. By thousands of voices, all over the earth, the warning will be given. Miracles will be wrought, the sick will be healed, and signs and wonders will follow the believers.

> I saw the latter rain was coming as the midnight cry [The Millerite Movement], and with *ten times the power*.[19]

Troubling moments in Adventist history

Whenever the true appears, Satan inevitably tries to counterfeit it. Spiritual gifts are no exception. Divine healing is easily distorted. Speaking in tongues is a natural target for fakery. Outbreaks of self-proclaimed prophets and apostles cause incredible difficulties.

Ellen White remarks that the more spectacular gifts are not common precisely because they are so easily counterfeited. Both Jesus (Matt. 24:24) and Paul (1 Thess. 5:19-21) registered cautions.

There have been periodic outbreaks of charismatic-type movements in Adventist history. In the years following 1844, the influence of Methodism was strong. Methodist camp meetings experienced outbreaks of being "slain in the Spirit," speaking in tongues, holy dancing, and other manifestations. Ellen White registers a number of fanatical incidents among early Adventists and former Millerites. Some people would roll "just like a hoop"; others believed in sinless perfection, exchanged wives, and advocated spiritual free love. Still others thought it wrong to work, believing the millennial Sabbath had begun. Yet others crept around on the floor like little children, supposedly to show their humility. Some danced and sang "glory, glory, glory" over and over again, while others jumped up and down with their hands raised for half an hour at a time. A few went at it so hard they were arrested and put in jail. She termed these manifestations "oddities and strange exercisings" that ought not to appear among God's people.[20]

Around the turn of the century, a charismatic revival known as the "holy flesh" movement broke out among Seventh-day Adventists. It was influenced by exaggerated views of sanctification deduced from some of the more radical views of A.T. Jones and E. J. Waggoner on sanctification and the Methodist holiness revivals prevalent at the time. Stephen Haskell reported that some Seventh-day Adventist ministers were preaching that it was wrong to kill insects, that you couldn't have the seal of God if you had even one gray hair, and that deformed persons could be healed if they were part of the 144,000.[21]

Spiritual gifts must always be governed and controlled by the revealed Word of God and must only be exercised within the boundaries set by the Bible. One of the problems with the contemporary charismatic movement is that people's subjective experience often replaces the Bible as the final authority in their lives. "The Holy Spirit works," Ellen White wrote, "in a manner that commends itself to the good judgment of the people."[22]

The Bible presents ample evidence for the perpetuity of spiritual gifts. The cessationist arguments devise artificial divisions of spiritual gifts based on hierarchies of importance that have no biblical backing. The Adventist church has experienced both true and counterfeit manifestations of spiritual gifts but remains committed to their continuing role in the life of the church.

Notes:

1. John F. MacArthur, Jr.,*Charismatic Chaos* (Grand Rapids: Zondervan Publishing House, 1992), 109. An otherwise excellent book on some excesses of the contemporary charismatic movement, MacArthur's book takes the

cessationist position on the power or sign gifts, including the gift of prophecy, though he allows for a gift of prophecy defined personally by him to fit his conception of what it ought to be (231, fn).

2. *Ibid*, 199.

3. For a good exposition of this point, see Wayne Grudem, *The Gift of Prophecy in the New Testament and Today* (Westchester, Ill.: Crossway Books, 1988), 227-252.

4. *Review and Herald*, Feb. 15, 1870.

5. Uriah Smith, "Do We Discard the Bible by Endorsing the Visions?" *Review and Herald*, Jan. 13, 1863.

6. L. H. Christian, *The Fruitage of Spiritual Gifts* (Washington, D.C.: Review and Herald Publishing Association, 1947), 17.

7. Carlyle B. Haynes, *The Gift of Prophecy*, Revised Edition (Nashville: Southern Publishing Association, 1946), 21.

8. A. G. Daniells, *The Abiding Gift of Prophecy* (Mountain View, Calif.: Pacific Press Publishing Association, 1936), 11.

9. Ellen G. White, *The Desire of Ages*, 823.

10. Ronald A. N. Kydd, *Charismatic Gifts in the Early Church* (Peabody, Mass.: Hendrickson Publishers, 1984), 4.

11. *Ibid*, 87.

12. For more information on this transformation, see William DeArteaga, *Quenching the Spirit* (Lake Mary, Fl.: Creation House, 1992) and James H. Rutz, *The Open Church* (Auburn, Maine: The SeedSowers, 1992).

13. Quoted in Kydd, 27.

14. Quoted in Daniells, 227.

15. William DeArteaga, *Quenching the Spirit* (Lake Mary, Fl.: Creation House, 1992), 64.

16. For a history of Irving, see Arnold Dallimore, *Forerunner of the Charismatic Movement* (Chicago: Moody Press, 1983.)

17. Dave MacPherson, *The Incredible Cover-Up* (Plainfield, N.J.: Logos International, 1975).

18. White, *The Great Controversy*, 611.
19. White, *The Great Controversy*, 612; *Spalding and Magan Collection*, 4.
20. White, *Selected Messages*, 2:26, 27; 3:371-373.
21. For information on charismatic movements within Adventism, see *Selected Messages*, 2:31-39 and George R. Knight, *From 1888 to Apostasy* (Hagerstown, Md.: Review and Herald Publishing Association, 1987), 167-171.
22. White, *Selected Messages*, 3:371.

FIVE

A Gift for Everyone

There is one gift that is available to everyone—a gift connected with what Paul calls "a more excellent way" (1 Cor. 13:1). That's the gift of love. Love is permanaent, while other gifts are transitory. Love is the "greatest," surpassing even hope and faith. Other spiritual gifts only work efficiently and effectively when encased in an atmosphere of love.

Edwin Markham's famous poem summarizes the power of love:

He drew a circle that shut me out;
Heretic, rebel, a thing to flout.
But love and I had a wit to win:
We drew a circle that took him in.

Consider, for instance . . .

The enemy party

She was the dark-eyed daughter of the village barber—small, stormy, an economy sized carbon copy of a movie star beauty, seen through the wrong end of a telescope. She was also the terror of the tiny tots and the ringleader of the "big kids" in the third grade.

Pat and Peggy, regular victims of the dark-eyed terror, came home crying almost daily. Determined to break this cycle, Dad came up with an idea. "Let's have a party." Pat and Peggy's tears dried up magically. Right away they got creative: "Ice cream, cake, big red balloons!" "And friends?" Dad added. The tears started again. "We don't have any friends," Pat blubbered. 'Nothing but enemies," wailed Peggy.

A rare inspiration hit Dad. "Let's have an enemy party. Let's invite all your enemies—especially the worst ones—and we'll fill 'em up with cake and ice cream and give 'em big red balloons to take home."

Peggy and Pat looked at each other and rolled their eyes in a "What's with Dad?" gesture.

The enemy party was a wild success. And the "terror of the tiny tots" had the best time of all. She ate ice cream and cake, got a big red balloon, and rolled on the floor in delight.

Pat and Peggy never came home crying again. Their greatest enemy became their greatest friend and protector.

One day the former terror's father dropped by and asked why she was invited to the party. "Well," Dad said, "She's a solid citizen who likes ice cream and cake, and big red balloons. Why not?"

"You know," her dad said, "No one ever invited her before. You have no idea what a difference it's made!" That enemy party had a lot of love mixed in with the ice cream, cake, and big red balloons.

Love—What is it?

"Love" is difficult to define. "I love chocolate cake," "I love to water ski," and "I love my spouse," don't all mean exactly the same thing.

On the other hand, as C. S. Lewis points out, any of these "human" loves may become a "god" when overindulged—and rapidly convert itself into a demon.[1]

Smiley Blanton used the word *lovability*.[2] It has two facets—how we are treated, and how we treat others. Assuming that our parents were good role models, Blanton says that we learn lovability in that family relationship. Therefore, "To be a lovable person in the deepest sense, it follows that we must re-create an adult version of the good qualities originally evolved in the relationship between mother and child."[3]

Arthur Spalding reflects on the law of love—Mark 10:42-45:

> Jesus called them together and said, "You know that those who are regarded as rulers of the Gentiles lord it over them, and their high officials exercise authority over them. Not so with you. Instead, whoever wants to become great among you must be your servant, and whoever wants to be first must be slave of all. For even the Son of Man did not come to be served, but to serve, and to give his life as a ransom for many."

Spalding asks the question about Jesus, "Loved whom?" Answer: Peter, with all his impetuous habits, Judas, even while he was stealing and plotting, James and John, even while they politicked for the highest position in the kingdom. "Love," Spalding wrote, "is Power. And we do well with a capital letter to personify it. For power is life, and life is love; and God is Love. The power that makes men over from their natural selves into godlike men, into children of God, is Love within, Christ within, God within."[4]

Leon Morris concludes his in-depth study on the concept of love in the Bible with these significant words:

> When we understand love in the light of the cross, we understand that love is to be shown to the unlovely and the unworthy. No one who takes the cross seriously can think otherwise. The Christian who has been transformed by God's love revealed in the cross cannot be other than deeply concerned for sinners. That is what love means. And as he responds to God's love he becomes a loving person. It is love that brought him life and therefore it is love that he brings to life.[5]

God, of course, "*is* love" (1 John 4:8). Our love, from whatever motivation it may stem, is what C. S Lewis calls "need-love." God's love, by contrast, is "gift-love." God *gave* His Son—He *gives* gifts to humanity.[6]

1 Corinthians 13

First Corinthians 13 points out that *agape*, the highest perception of love envisioned in the Greek language, is more than a *charismata*—a gift. It is a realm or context within which the other *charismata* are practiced.[7] This *agape* is the thinking pattern of the renewed, born-again mind (2 Cor. 5:17; Rom. 12:2). It is more than behavior. It is an attitude that produces a type of behavior that makes a Christian a "living letter" (2 Cor. 3:2). Schatzmann observes:

> In the context of 1 Cor. 12–14, however, Paul accepted love alone as the realm in which gifts were to function in their diversity. Outside *agape*, any charismatic function was unable to upbuild the community. In fact, the opposite would be accomplished; the unity of the body would be destroyed because of divisiveness, and the growth of the body would be stunted.[8]

So Paul argues that the practice of *charismata* outside the framework of love demonstrates spiritual immaturity. The practice of sign gifts such as martyrdom (vs. 3), or leadership gifts such as faith and administration, are of little merit unless encased in an attitude of love (vs. 2). 1 Cor. 13 lists eight things love is or does, and seven things it is not or does not do:

What love is and does:

Love is patient, is kind, searches for truth, holds up under pressure, always believes the best, looks to the future—not the past, and is consistent.

What love is not or does not do:

Love is not jealous, does not brag, does not embarrass others, is not arrogant, is not selfish, does not remember a wrong suffered, and does not anger easily.

What are the implications of these characteristics for the application and utilization of spiritual gifts? First, everyone will realize that all spiritual gifts are of equal importance. If wrapped in love, the person with the gift of helps will not envy the person with the gift of evangelism just because he or she gets more public exposure. The high-profile public speaker, on the other hand, won't embarrass others, act arrogantly, or anger easily.

When things get rough in the church and interpersonal relationships are strained, an environment of love manifests patient and kindness, searches for truth, holds up under pressure, looks to the future rather than the past, and is consistent. That's a tall order, possible only through the power of the Holy Spirit; nevertheless, it's the way of the Christian lifestyle.

The fruit of the Spirit

Another indicator of a Christian personality is the list of characteristics in Gal. 5:22, 23: "But the fruit of the Spirit is love, joy, peace, patience, kindness, goodness, faithfulness, gentleness and self-control. Against such things there is no law." Notice that the word is *fruit* (singular) of the Spirit, not *fruits* (plural). The Lord's ideal is that *all* these characteristics be present in an individual all the time. Peter presents another list of traits (2 Pet. 1:3-11). He introduces his list with the phrase "add to," connecting each characteristic until one reaches "love" at the top of the ladder. Actually, the Greek word *epichoregeo*, translated *add*, means "to supply," or "minister to," so this is not a chronological sequence but a set of characteristics that flow out of a person's life and result in an environment of love.

The Sermon on the Mount (Matt. 5–7) is another exposition of Christian virtues and attitudes, synonymous with a proper interpretation and application of the Ten Commandments. The application of these principles is built around Jesus' phrase, "You have heard that it was said. . . . But I tell you . . ."

These various lists deal primarily with the personality characteristics of an individual Christian and how that one person relates to the creation of an atmosphere of love.

The corporate perspective—"one another"

There is also a corporate set of reciprocal relationships that help create an atmosphere of love in the church. The Greek word *allelon* means "reciprocal," or "mutual"—usually translated "one another." The practice of these reciprocal relationships produces an atmosphere of love in a congregation.

INTER-RELATIONSHIPS	MUTUAL EDIFICATION	MUTUAL SERVICE	NEGATIVE COMMANDS
Love one another	Build one another up	Be servants to one another	Do not judge one another
Receive one another	Teach one another	Bear one another's burdens	Do not speak evil of one another
Greet one another	Exhort one another	Use hospitality toward one another	Do not murmur against one another
Have the same care for one another	Admonish one another	Be kind to one another	Do not bite and devour one another
Submit to one another	Speak to one another in songs and psalms	Pray for one another	Do not provoke one another
Forbear one another			Do not envy one another
Confess your sins to one another			Do not lie to one another
Forgive one another			

Rom. 12:1-5—the "measure of faith"

In these verses, Paul combines an analogy of the human body with the concept of a "measure of faith," declaring that a renewed mind can override "the pattern of this world" and understand God's will. This process, however, demands "sober judgment."

He begins the passage with the word *therefore*, indicating an application derived from what he said previously. Members are admonished to present their "bodies" as spiritual sacrifices. This doesn't primarily deal with healthful living (as important as that is). In the previous chapter, Paul has discussed how ancient Israelites sacrificed part of their body through circumcision, but Christians are called on to do more than that. Total dedication is an element of "spiritual worship." It involves a complete "renewing of the mind"—a new way of thinking that allows a person to perceive the "good, pleasing, perfect will of God." This attitude allows for "sober judgment" on oneself. The objective standard that determines "sober" judgment is the "measure of faith" given each person by the Lord.

The word *faith* is usually associated with the saving faith that is part of the new-birth process, or to taking God at His word and exercising "faith" when the going gets rough and one can't see the end from the beginning. In this case, however, the phrase "measure of faith" is a synonym for spiritual gifts.[9] Verses 6-8 list a number of spiritual gifts, and verses 9-21 summarize behavioral attitudes and actions that help create an atmosphere of love within which the gifts can function. Paul attaches no hierarchy of value to any spiritual gift—all are of equal importance. They all constitute assorted tools used to accomplish the work of the Kingdom. This perspective places everyone on the same level and focuses them on accomplishing the will of God.

Spiritual gifts and church unity

In 1 Cor. 12, Paul outlines the way in which spiritual gifts serve to unify the church. Unity is a much-abused and misunderstood word. To some people, unity means "everyone agrees with me." To others, it means that everyone will believe and behave exactly the same way—a perspective called uniformity. To yet others, it means that even if we don't agree on everything, we still get along and learn to live with each other as fellow travelers on the road to heaven. Most instances of disunity in the church don't have to do with doctrinal differences—they involve differences over procedures and personal likes and dislikes.

Paul's argument for unity draws on an analogy of the unity of the human body. The unpresentable parts of the body, he says, receive special honor. The presentable parts, on the other hand, need no special treatment, because they are already honored. His conclusion: "God has combined the members of the body and has given greater honor to the parts that lacked it, so that there should be no division in the body, but that its parts should have equal concern for each other." Therefore:

- The Holy Spirit is given for the common good, vs. 7.
- The parts of the body should have equal concern for each other, vs. 25.
- If one parts suffers, all suffer, vs. 25.
- If one part is honored, all rejoice, vs. 25.

The framework of love, then, becomes the environment within which spiritual gifts can operate efficiently and effectively. "Gift-love", to use C. S Lewis' term, answers the cry of "needs-love." The individual and corporate Christian personalities evident in people who are in truth "living epistles" generate ministry and result in a united congregation dedicated to the advancement of the kingdom.

Notes:

1. C. S. Lewis, *The Four Loves* (New York: Harcourt Brace Jovanovich, Publishers, 1960), 11-21.
2. Smiley Blanton, *Love or Perish* (Greenwich, Conn.: Fawcett Publications, 1956).

3. *Ibid.*, 144.

4. Arthur W. Spalding, *Who Is the Greatest?* (Mountain View, Calif.: Pacific Press Publishing Association, 1941), 41.

5. Leon Morris, *Testaments of Love* (Grand Rapids, Mich.: William B. Eerdmans Publishing Company, 1981), 278. This is one of the most exhaustive studies done on the word *love* in the Bible. Well worth reading.

6. *Ibid.*

7. Siegfried Schatzmann, *A Pauline Theology of Charismata* (Peabody, Mass.: Hendrickson Publishers, 1987), 47.

8. *Ibid*, 48.

9. For further information , see Charles R. Erdman, *The Epistle of Paul to the Romans* (Philadelphia: The Westminster Press), and *The Seventh-day Adventist Bible Commentary*, 6:618.

SIX

Support Gifts

The Holy Spirit has placed a number of spiritual gifts in the church that are unspectacular and "quiet." These gifts—helps, mercy, exhortation or encouragement, giving, hospitality, and service—form the underpinnings of a church's ministry. In most churches, a significant percentage of the members will have gifts that fall into this category.

Members with these gifts are those who do the everyday work of the church. They greet at the church door, run the community service program, prepare fellowship meals, visit people in the hospital, spend time talking with people who need counsel, and minister to those going through difficult times. They support the church with financial help and in general make the church's program function effectively. They are often unsung heroes who receive little or no recognition for the vital part they play. They are the ones who often say, "I'm *just* a [whatever job they do] in the church." Without that "just a . . . ," however, the church would be a poorer place and its ministry far less effective.

Relationships, relationships!

The support gifts are the underpinnings of an incarnational ministry. Incarnational ministry means that the teachings of the gospel are embodied in the lives and ministry of the people who profess to believe them, and the transmission of the gospel takes place through people. In Paul's words: "You show that you are a letter from Christ, the result of our ministry, written not with ink but with the Spirit of the living God, not on tablets of stone but on tablets of human hearts" (2 Corinthians 3:3).

In 2 Corinthians 5:18-20, Paul likens incarnational ministry to an ambassadorship:

> All this is from God, who reconciled us to himself through Christ and gave us the ministry of reconciliation: that God was reconciling the world to himself in Christ, not counting men's sins against them. And he has committed to us the message of reconciliation. We are therefore Christ's ambassadors, as though God were making his appeal through us. We implore you on Christ's behalf: Be reconciled to God.

The reconciliation originates with God, but it comes to people's attention through us. Ambassadors represent their country in another land. When you walk into your country's embassy in another land, you literally walk into a parcel of your own country. The flag becomes the seal and guarantee of protection and help provided by the country in which you hold citizenship. Christians, therefore, represent to a fallen world the ambassadorship of the earth made new—the Kingdom of God.

The gift of helps

Definition: *The gift of helps is the special ability God gives to some members of the body of Christ to invest the talents they have in the life and ministry of other members of the body, thus enabling the person helped to increase the effectiveness of his or her spiritual gifts.*[1]

People with this gift usually have unselfish natures and like to do small things, even menial tasks, with no thought of receiving credit. They do them for the joy of doing the job and knowing they are serving the Lord and the church. They often take on tasks that allow the leadership gifts in the church to be enhanced.

Barnabas and the gift of helps

Barnabas is an example of a person with this gift. In Acts 4, he appears as a landowner who sells property to help finance the work of the infant church. In Acts 9, it is he who takes the newly converted Saul to the other disciples and convinces them to accept him as a brother. In Acts 11, he makes the trip to Tarsus in search of Saul and inaugurates him into ministry at the church in Antioch. In Acts 13, he and Paul are set aside for the Gentile mission of the church, and he becomes Paul's principal mentor. In Acts 13:42, the expression changes from "Barnabas and Saul" to "Paul and Barnabas." The Bible registers no complaint on his part. When he and Paul have a falling out over the value of Mark as a missionary, Barnabas once more chooses the route that allows him to build someone up—and stays with Mark (Acts 15). Apparently he did a good job, since Paul later valued Mark's ministry (2 Tim. 4:11).

The Gift of Mercy

All Christians should be tenderhearted and show compassion for those who are less fortunate. The Seventh-day Adventist Church spends vast sums of money and utilizes vast amounts of human resources in helping people. I once attended two Community Service congresses in Papua New Guinea and the Solomon Islands. Four to five thousand people attended each congress. They marched, sang songs, and displayed crafts. Some had arrived weeks prior to the congresses and planted gardens for food, waiting for the congress to begin. But the highlight of both congresses was the reports about the incredible things being done in their community service programs. Literally thousands of people—often entire villages—were affected by these dedicated men and women with support gifts. It was awe-inspiring to see such dedication.

Definition: *The gift of mercy is the special ability that God gives to certain members of the body of Christ to feel genuine empathy and compassion for individuals, both Christian and non-Christian, who suffer distressing physical, mental or emotional problems, and to translate that compassion into* *cheerfully done deeds that reflect Christ's love and alleviate the suffering.*

Jesus outlined the characteristics of those with this gift in Matt. 25:34-40. Notice that the people addressed in this text didn't even realize they had helped so many or how or when the Lord took note of their actions.

Characteristics of the gift of mercy

Those who have this gift usually display the following characteristics:

- Tears come easily when they see or hear things that sadden them.
- Most people perceive that they have an empathetic personality.
- They want to help out and help people in misery.
- They are unusually sympathetic to the hurts of others.
- People in need like to have them around, because they cheer them up.
- They are not easily repulsed by the sight of miserable people but usually think, "How can I help?"

The gift of exhortation or encouragement

This is a person-centered gift, one of the few gifts directly commanded in the Bible (Heb. 3:13). The KJV reads, "Exhort one another daily"; the NIV says, "Encourage one another daily."

Definition: *The gift of exhortation is the special ability that God gives to certain members of the body of Christ to minister words of comfort, consolation, encouragement, and counsel to other members of the body in such a way that they feel helped and healed.*

People with this gift spend time with individuals and help them through difficult situations. They have the ability to cheer people up just by talking to them. They bring out biblical principles for relationships, showing how they can help people, and individuals go away feeling better. Encouragers usually dedicate themselves to short-term help and encouragement. Long-term help is usually done by those with the gift of pastoring.

The example of Barnabas

Once again, Barnabas is an example of a person with this gift. His name means "son of encouragement." If it were not for Barnabas' gift of encouragement, we might be missing almost half of the New Testament—thirteen letters by Paul, and the Gospel of Mark. It was he who encouraged both authors and kept them working through some very hard times.

People who have this gift usually exhibit the following characteristics:

- They frequently advise others about various things.
- People take their counsel and advice seriously because they feel helped.
- People like to be around them because they cheer them up by their simple attitude and demeanor and down-to-earth advice.
- People learn from them how to apply "theoretical" Christianity to real-life situations.
- They enjoy sharing their personal testimony with people because they know God will use it to encourage and help others.

The gift of giving

All Christians are expected to be faithful to the Lord with tithes and offerings, and to do so cheerfully (2 Cor. 9:7). Some Christians, however, receive a special gift from the Lord enabling them to give extraordinary amounts of financial help to the Lord's work.

Definition: *The gift of giving is the special ability that God gives to certain members of the Body of Christ to contribute their material resources to the work of the Lord with liberality and cheerfulness.*

Luke 6:38: "Give, and it will be given to you. A good measure, pressed down, shaken together and running over, will be poured into your lap. For with the measure you use, it will be measured to you" is a promise from the Lord, but it is also a description of the attitude of a person with the gift of giving. In Romans 12:8, Paul uses the word *generously* as the identifying mark of this gift. Ellen White remarks:

> Give what you can now, and as you co-operate with Christ, your hand will open to impart still more. And God will refill your hand, that the treasure of truth may be taken to many souls. He will give to you that you may give to others.

This is exactly what happens to people with this gift.

The Greek word for giving in these verses is *didomi*. In its various connotations, it means to give throughout, to give away oneself, to give over and above, and to hand over. It is often qualified by the phrase *en aploteti*, which means to give with liberality, with purity, and in sincerity.

This gift is not limited to rich people. Notice how Paul recounts the willing spirit of the Macedonian members:

> And now, brothers, we want you to know about the grace that God has given the Macedonian churches. Out of the most severe trial, their overflowing joy and their extreme poverty welled up in rich generosity. For I testify that they gave as much as they were able, and even beyond their ability. Entirely on their own, they urgently pleaded with us for the privilege of sharing in this service to the saints. And they did not do as we expected, but they gave themselves first to the Lord and then to us in keeping with God's will (2 Cor. 8:1-5).

Someone with the gift of giving led these members to share not only material means, but the spirit that accompanies spiritually-oriented stewardship.

Captain Merle Hyde owned a fishing business on an island in the Caribbean. He called me one day to make an urgent visit to the town where he lived. "I have," he said, "something to show you, and it's urgent that you get here right away."

I flew to the islands. Captain Merle picked me up at the airport, and as we traversed the muddy, rutted road toward the town, he recounted the stories he had told me before of how the Lord blessed him so much he couldn't give his money away to the church fast enough.

"He always puts it back," he said, "faster than I can give it away."

As we pulled into the town, he pointed to some buildings and said, "Well, there it is, I called you here to get it going!"

I nearly fainted. Captain Merle had built and equipped an entire school plant, everything from classrooms to desks and offices.

"OK," he said, "let's go sign the papers turning the school over to the conference, and you go get the teachers. School starts in a few weeks."

"Captain Merle," I asked, "How can you afford this?"

"Oh," he said, "that's nothing—the Lord put it back before I could even finish the school, and now I'm trying to figure out what to do next."

That's the gift of giving!

How the gift of giving benefits the Lord's work

People with this gift intuitively recognize the material needs of others. They don't have a "me-first" attitude, but rather a God-given ability to obtain significant financial resources, a large portion of which are then passed on to the Lord's work. They also have a conviction that whatever they have belongs to the Lord. They consider themselves stewards of His goods and a channel for using them for the benefit of others.

According to the New Testament, the financial means returned to the Lord's work by those who have this gift are used: (1) to meet the needs of believers within the local church itself (Gal. 6:10; 1 John 3:17; 1 Tim. 5:3 -5); (2) to meet the needs of believers in other local churches (2 Cor. 8:1-6; Rom. 15:25, 26); (3) to meet the needs of those using their gifts of leadership in full-time ministry for the Lord (Phil. 4:10-19; 1 Cor. 9:1-14; 1 Tim. 5:17, 18), and (4) to meet the needs of non-believers (Gal. 6:10).

The gifts of hospitality and service

Of all the support gifts, these two may be the most pivotal. People with these gifts know how to make other people feel comfortable, accepted and wanted. They are the ones willing to take people home for a meal, and find ways to make them feel part of the family. People with the gift of hospitality ought to make up the core of greeters or receptionists at the door of your church on Sabbath morning.

The gift of hospitality

The gift of hospitality is one of those implied in the New Testament, not directly included in any of the lists. The key passage is 1 Peter 4:9: "Offer hospitality to one another without grumbling." Verse 10 immediately speaks of spiritual gifts. Matt. 25:35, Heb. 13:2, 3 John 5-8 are other texts that allude to the gift of hospitality. The Greek word for hospitality, *philoxenia*, means "expressing love to a visitor or stranger."

Definition: *The gift of hospitality is the special ability that God gives to certain members of the body of Christ to provide open arms, open house and warm welcome for those in need of friendship, a warm welcome, food and lodging.*

The same Captain Merle who had the gift of giving, also had the gift of hospitality. Arriving at his hometown one day for a preaching appointment, I was on my way to the small hotel near the airport when he arrived.

"You can't stay at that hotel anymore," he informed me. "We have a new plan." Arriving at his new house, recently completed, he informed me that, following the example of the Shunammite lady in 2 Kings 4, he had built a special room on his house reserved for conference personnel when they visited the island. Once again, I stood with my mouth open while Captain Merle put his spiritual gifts to work!

The gift of service

The gift of service, or "ministering," as it is translated in the KJV, comes from the Greek word *diakonia*, translated "deacon." It is mentioned in Romans 12:7: "If it is serving, let him serve . . ." in the sense of the ministration of those who show Christian affection through help and caring.

Definition: *The gift of service is the special ability that God gives to certain members of the body of Christ to identify unmet needs involved in a task related to God's work, and to make use of available resources.*

This gift is not limited to those who serve in the office of deacon, although those chosen for this office ought to have it. The office of deacon was initiated in the New Testament over the issue of food distribution and how to best care for the needs of widows (Acts 6). In addition to this task, however, the people chosen to be deacons also had other gifts such as evangelism, faith, and wisdom (Acts 6:3-6).

Election to the office of deacon doesn't necessarily mean that one has the gift of service. It is all too easy to confuse a church office with automatic giftedness. As we will see in later chapters, a church ought to take into account spiritual giftedness as well as availability or seniority in choosing its leaders.

The job description for deacons (and deaconesses) in the Seventh-day Adventist *Church Manual* includes many of the elements involved in the gift of service, though in practice the office is all too often limited to taking care of the church building and general supervision of physical needs on Sabbath morning.

Summary

The effective functioning of support gifts is all-important to the life and ministry of the church. They are the most common, and are the underpinning of the relationship program of the church congregation. When these are not functioning, the church becomes deficient in its very lifeblood.

Notes:

1. Unless otherwise noted, the definitions of spiritual gifts are taken from C. Peter Wagner, *Your Spiritual Gifts Can Help Your Church Grow*, rev. ed. (Ventura, Calif.: Regal Books, 1994). Used by permission.

SEVEN

Teaching Gifts

The spiritual gifts that fall under the category of teaching are profoundly valuable in the life of the church. They are also some of the most underutilized. Many churches have no systematic religious education system, other than the short time spent in Sabbath School.[1] General Conference statistics tell us that 90 percent of the world membership of the church learn about the Scriptures, the beliefs of the church, and the Christian life at the local church level. This fact alone makes it extremely important that the teaching gifts be utilized to the maximum. Beyond the internal teaching is the teaching that takes place in seminar evangelism, baptismal classes, small group Bible studies, and midweek church services.

The gifts of wisdom and knowledge are related to the specific spiritual gift of teaching. The gift of pastor or shepherding is also related to teaching, because it often function as the catalyst for an effective teaching ministry.

The gift of teaching

Definition: *The gift of teaching is the special ability that God gives to some members of the body of Christ to communicate information relevant to the health and ministry of the body and its members in such a way that others will learn.*

The gift of teaching implies more than an individual instructing a few more individuals. It implies the utilization of this gift to set up a teaching ministry in the church. This teaching ministry includes curricula that lead to increasing spirituality and personal Christian maturity—and skill-building for Christian service.

The main characteristics of people with the gift of teaching are:

- People will constantly understand truth as a result of their teaching.
- The teacher will have an intense desire to understand truth and will excel in the ability to explain it to others.
- People with this gift are not satisfied with unclear or obscure meanings. They will work at it until the truth is clear and easily understood.
- People progress in knowledge and understanding as a result of the work of these gifted teachers.

The teaching ministry of the church

Stanley S. Will records a story told him by a conference president.

> "When I was a young fellow," the conference president related, "there were five of us in a particular Sabbath School class. I regret to say we were ogres to teach. It seems we were continually trying to do something to disrupt the teacher or to disrupt one another, but our Sabbath School teacher was patient. She visited us in our homes, talked to us about our personal experience with the Lord, and planned socials for us. There are five of us in the work now—one is a conference president, two are principals in our schools, one is a minister, and one is a local elder. I am sure that all of us give much credit to that Sabbath School teacher."[2]

That story could be repeated over and over again.

The Great Commission in Matt. 28:20 specifically points out that teaching is a key responsibility of the church: "Teaching them to obey everything I have commanded you . . ." Teaching gifts are given as a means of communicating spiritual truth to church members and non-church members alike.

Ellen White on a teaching ministry

Ellen White emphasizes the importance of a teaching ministry: "There should be less preaching, and more teaching. There are those who want more definite light than they receive from hearing the sermons."[3]

Elder William White asked his mother to explain what she meant. "I have heard you say, Mother, that we should have more teaching and less preaching, less preaching and more teaching—speaking of the matter of getting the people together and having Bible readings." Her answer: "That was the way in Christ's day; He would speak to the people, and they would call out a question as to what it meant. He was a teacher of the people." William's further question was: "Then at one time I remember very distinctly about your saying, that 'as we approach nearer the end, I have seen our campmeetings with less preaching and more Bible study; little groups all over the ground with their Bibles in their hands, and different ones leading out in a free conversational study of the Scriptures.'" Her answer: "There are those that want more definite light. There are some that take longer time to get hold of things, and get what you really mean. If they could have the privilege of having it made a little plainer, they would see that, and catch hold of that, and it would be like a nail fastened in a sure place, and it would be written on the tablets of their hearts."[4]

Jesus' teaching ministry

Jesus set an example of a teaching ministry. Of the ninety times He is addressed directly in the Gospels, He is called "rabbi" sixty times. "Rabbi" is the Greek equivalent of the Aramaic (Jesus' mother tongue) word for "sir," but is commonly used in the sense of "my teacher."[5] Of the remaining thirty times, He is commonly addressed as a *didaskolos*, the Greek word for teacher. Jesus, "as his custom was," spent time teaching (Mark 10:1), acknowledged the title of teacher (John 13:13), taught in the synagogues (Matt. 9:35) and from village to village (Mark 6:6).

Paul's teaching ministry

Paul also spent a great deal of time teaching.

> Paul entered the synagogue and spoke boldly there for three months, arguing persuasively about the kingdom of God. But some of them became obstinate—they refused to believe and publicly maligned the Way. So Paul left them. He took the disciples with him and had discussions daily in the lecture hall of Tyrannus. This went on for two years, so that all the Jews and Greeks who lived in the province of Asia heard the word of the Lord.—Acts 19:8-10.

Calculating the number of hours probably spent in class, these students received the equivalent of a junior college education in theology and soul winning from Paul.

Teaching techniques

Teaching is done in various ways. In some church communions, people learn a particular set of beliefs through a catechism. This type of teaching is usually based on a question-and-answer format, the answers being self-evident from the questions themselves and usually learned by rote memory.

Church members are called to do more than memorize certain doctrinally oriented answers, however. They are admonished to understand and "test" whatever they learn to make sure it is biblically correct and well understood. Paul commended the Bereans because "they received the message with great eagerness and examined the Scriptures every day to see if what Paul said was true" (Acts 17:11).

The teaching techniques of Jesus

Jesus broke with the catechism methodology used in the synagogues of His time (Matt. 7:29). The scribes and Pharisees used a dogmatic teaching system based on memorizing the opinions of great past rabbis. The system focused on rigid rules prescribed for every act, down to the smallest details of life. Under the synagogue teachers, the youth were instructed in the countless regulations which, as orthodox Israelites, they were expected to observe.[6]

Jesus took a different approach. Rather than lists of requirements learned by rote memory, He went from the known to the unknown and stimulated people's minds by presenting truth through the agency of their most familiar associations.

1. He asked people to listen to Him, announcing to villages that He was about to enter and teach.

2. His body language attracted attention. "When he was set . . . ," He assumed the typical posture of an oriental teacher (Matt. 5:1).

3. He spoke in pictorial, imaginative, yet concrete language that people understood. For example, to fishermen, He said, "I will make you fishers of men."

4. He taught inductively, using the familiar to explain the unfamiliar. He used, Ellen White tells us, illustrations in His teaching which called into activity the hearers' most hallowed recollections and sympathies, that He might reach the inner temple of the soul.[7]

5. He got to the point without making His teaching too complicated.

6. His demeanor and body language told people they were important to Him and that He was paying attention to them.

The gift of knowledge

The gift of knowledge has to do with the discovery of truth. Some people have been given the ability to dig deep and accumulate a reservoir of knowledge about the Scriptures and the way of salvation that is invaluable to the work of the church.

Definition: *The gift of knowledge is the special ability that God gives to some members of the body of Christ to discover, accumulate, analyze, and clarify information and ideas that are pertinent to the growth of the church and the well-being of the body.*

All Christians should build up a knowledge of the Scriptures and a store of biblical information. All Christians need to know about prophecy, biblical and church history, and the doctrines of the church. Jesus told His disciples that they had received the "knowledge of the secrets of the kingdom of heaven" (Matt. 13:11). Paul called this general understanding of the principles of the kingdom the "fragrance of the knowledge of God" (2 Cor. 2:14). It is this knowledge that leads to Christian maturity (Eph. 4:13).

The gift of knowledge, however, goes deeper. Those with this gift usually have the ability to organize their minds so that their storehouse of knowledge becomes useful, not just theoretical. Sometimes, the gifts of teaching and knowledge are combined so that the recipient becomes a scholar-teacher. Widely read, they know how to connect bits and pieces of information so that they make a logical whole.

Books, reading, and study

Persons with the gift of knowledge will read extensively. They will know how to use Bible dictionaries, encyclopedias, commentaries, and handbooks. They will know how to do an accurate exegesis of a biblical passage and how to dig out its historical and cultural backgrounds. They will dig into history books and be at least conversant with what is going on in the theological world.

The following chart shows aspects of the gift of knowledge:

Luke 1:1-4	Luke checked out sources and outlined his material in an orderly way.
Acts 18:24, 25	Apollos had a deep fund of knowledge and taught about Jesus "accurately."
Rom. 15:14	Knowledge develops competence to teach.
2 Cor. 11:6	Those with this gift are not necessarily trained speakers.

More than information

Sometimes a person who is a scholar—a walking encyclopedia of knowledge—may need to team up with someone who has the gift of teaching. Transmitting information, no matter how valuable, may make no impact at all. A friend of mine once went to hear a renowned historian give a lecture. He had read all the historian's books, followed his career with dedication, and considered it a great privilege to finally hear the man in person. Fifteen minutes into the lecture, he realized his mistake. The presentation was dry as the hills of Gilboa—disorganized, irrelevant, and just plain boring. People were leaving by the droves. He stuck it out to the bitter end, but, he told me, it was a struggle. This lecturer may have been a deep reservoir of information, but as a communicator, the presenter left a lot to be desired.

Zeal without knowledge

"Unless our knowledge is a stepping-stone to the accomplishment of the highest purposes," Ellen White reminds us, "it is worthless."[8] Some people have neither the gift of teaching nor a fund of knowledge, yet hold major teaching positions. These teachers usually pass on personal opinion rather than biblical knowledge. Personal opinion may be interesting, and even helpful, but it is not the same as imparting biblical principles and then applying them to life. As we have pointed out in other places, giftedness is useful only if it comes through a Christian personality. Sometimes a person with some knowledge gets "puffed up" (1 Cor. 8:1). When this happens, the valuable information they could share is lost in the fog of their self-centered attitudes.

The gift of wisdom

Wisdom is the ability to use knowledge in a practical way. When the Bible says, "The fear of the Lord—that is wisdom" (Prov. 28:28), it means that understanding what God is all about will lead to a practical application in everyday life.

Definition: *The gift of wisdom is the special ability that God gives to certain members of the body of Christ to know the* *mind of the Holy Spirit in such a way as to receive insight into how knowledge may best be applied to specific needs arising in the body of Christ.*

Wisdom takes bits and pieces of knowledge and puts them together in a way that makes them practical in everyday life. The book of Proverbs is an example of biblical wisdom. In the Old Testament—especially the books of Job, Psalms, Proverbs, and Ecclesiastes—wisdom is perceived as the "fear of the Lord." The Hebrew word for wisdom, *chakham*, is a holistic term that includes all of life and its activities—but always connected to God as its originator. It is distinguished from knowledge, understanding, or comprehension, in that it represents a higher degree of discernment and insight. It is always a relational term that asks the question "wisdom about what, or about whom, or wisdom from where?" In Job 28 and Prov. 1 and 8, it is personified and becomes a living entity rather than an abstraction.

Wisdom and knowledge

Knowledge is often thought of as the sum total of the information accumulated by an individual. In the biblical perspective, knowledge is incomplete without wisdom, just as teaching is incomplete without knowledge. Psalm 107:27-29 is an example. Skilled sailors "reeled and staggered like drunken men; they were at their wits' end." Knowledge of sailing was not enough in this kind of storm. "Then they cried out to the Lord in their trouble, and he brought them out of their distress." Calling on the Lord is the essence of wisdom, and it produced the desired effect: "He stilled the storm to a whisper; the waves of the sea were hushed."

The gift of wisdom supplies insights for the application of knowledge. The gift of teaching is the vehicle that communicates both information and application to students.

The gift of pastoring or shepherding

The word *pastor* comes from the Greek word *poimen*, which means "shepherd."

Definition: *The gift of pastor is the special ability that*

God gives to certain members of the body of Christ to assume a long-term personal responsibility for the spiritual welfare of a group of believers.

The gift of pastor is a bit more complex than some gifts, because we tend to perceive the gift of pastor and the office of pastor as synonymous. The concept of the ministry of all believers, however, assumes a distinction between the *office* of pastor and the *gift* of pastor. The gift of pastoring, or shepherding, involves personal spiritual care for a number of other Christians. The office of pastor is a position held by a person who may have spiritual gifts other than that of pastoring. The confusion comes about because we use one word to mean two different things.

The gift of pastoring—personal care for members of the church and others—serves as a catalyst for a teaching ministry. Those with the gift of pastoring open doors, prepare the way, provide materials, and prepare minds to receive the teaching of the church. The gift of pastoring is almost always combined with other spiritual gifts such as evangelism, teaching, etc.

Summary

The gifts of teaching, knowledge, wisdom, and pastoring enhance the ministry of the church by passing on religious information, applying it to everyday life, and showing its validity and usefulness. Those with the gift of pastoring serve as catalysts and open doors for the teaching ministry. Many people in a congregation may have the spiritual gift of pastoring. They should be utilized to the maximum.

Notes:

1. Religious education, in this chapter, refers to the educational system in the local church, not to the Seventh-day Adventist school system.

2. Stanley S. Will, *Teach* (Nashville: Southern Publishing Association, 1974), 23.

3. Ellen G. White, *Gospel Workers*, 407. A similar statement appears in *Evangelism*, 338.
4. *Spiritual Advancement the Object of Camp-Meetings*, 1897, 41, 42. This pamphlet is included on the Ellen White Writings CD-Rom produced by the White Estate.
5. W. E. Vine, *The Expanded Vine's Expository Dictionary of New Testament Words* (Minneapolis: Bethany House Publishers, 1984).
6. White, *The Desire of Ages*, 84
7. *Manuscript Releases,* vol. 13, 242.
8. White, *Fundamentals of Christian Education*, 541.

EIGHT

Leadership and Administrative Gifts

Leadership and administrative gifts are those that deal with the overall management and supervision of the church. A person with one or more of these gifts will be in the forefront of church administration and activity. Four gifts fall into this category: leadership, administration, apostleship, and faith. At first glance, the gift of faith may seem out of place here, but the point will be clarified as we proceed.

What is a "leader"?

From a biblical perspective, a leader is a person with a God-given capacity and responsibility to influence a specific group of God's people so that the group can fulfil God's purpose for its members. There are four significant points in this definition:

1. A God-given capacity means that the leader is gifted, either through natural talents or special gifts given by the Holy Spirit, in a specific way. Because of that giftedness, the leader can influence the group in a significant manner.

2. Leaders must feel a God-given sense of responsibility. They must feel accountable for those whom they influence.

3. Leadership is not exercised in a vacuum. It is directed toward a particular group or a particular task.

4. The leader must be convinced of what the Lord's will is for the group.

Leadership implies responsibility, a high degree of discipleship, and emotional stability. A leader's stress level can be very high at times. Christian leaders, nevertheless, are working for the Lord and for the advancement of His Kingdom. In spite of problems and setbacks, they will find ways and means to get the job done.

A church leader basically has two jobs—to model a strong spiritual example, and to create a climate where each person can do his or her best work.

The human factor

In a Christian context, the success of a ministry is to a great extent dependent on the Christian personality of the leader. Robert Pierson wrote:

> People are more important than methods, more essential than plans and policies. The success of any organization or project is more dependent upon the human factor than upon the budget factor or any other factor. With the right kind of leader a conference, a field, an institution will grow and develop despite obstacles and problems.[1]

The blurb on the back cover of a book by Calvin Rock sounds this message loud and clear:

> To be a successful administrator—you need to emphasize planning, performance, and evaluation. Right? Wrong. [The author] sees personal integrity—virtues such as self-control, loyalty, and disinterested love—as the key to administrative effectiveness.[2]

The example of Jesus

Jesus is the model for Christian leadership. From Jesus, leaders learn the power of kindness and the magic of understanding. Jesus never displayed a trace of harshness or rudeness. With His help, the Christian leader can rid his life of these traits. Like his master, the Christian leader approaches his problems in a spirit of love and Christlikeness.

Robert Pierson makes a significant statement on this point:

> One does not become a spiritual leader by birth, nor by social rank, nor by education. Spirituality is not bestowed upon an individual by a conference committee or a church board. Spiritual leadership comes by the power of the Holy Spirit. It comes though prayer, tears, and confession of sin. It requires a great deal of heart-searching and sacrifice. But only as we become spiritual workers can our leadership deliver the spiritual image so important to success.[3]

The apostle Peter sums up what we are talking about in these words:

> Therefore, prepare your minds for action; . . . Now that you have purified yourselves by obeying the truth so that you have sincere love for your brothers, love one another deeply, from the heart. . . . Show proper respect to everyone: love the brotherhood of believers, fear God, honor the king (1 Pet. 1: 13, 22; 2:17).

Servant leadership

The Bible advocates a leadership philosophy called "servant" leadership. Servant leadership produces in people a feeling of respect and love for a leader because he is doing the will of God and obviously has the best interests of his followers at heart. Peter Wagner writes:

> The people will know intuitively whether or not the [leader] loves them. It is a feeling produced by the Holy Spirit Himself within the church. The secular world knows nothing about this, but the church cannot get along without it.[4]

Servant leadership was exemplified by Jesus in His incarnation, as outlined in Phil. 2:1-11. Paul explains in this passage that our attitude should be the same as that of Jesus, who being God, gave up His position in heaven, laid aside His divine prerogatives, and took the form of a servant. He "emptied" Himself and identified with humanity to the point of crucifixion.

The key Greek word for servant is *doulos*, which also means "slave." A true Christian leader is a voluntary "slave" to Jesus and to those whom he or she serves. (See Rom. 1:1; 1 Cor. 9:19). This perspective on leadership produces an attitude of servanthood on the part of the leader. The chart below outlines some key concepts of servant leadership:

TEXT	PRINCIPLE
Jn. 13:35	"All men will know that you are my disciples, if you love one another."
Mk. 9:33-35	It is serving, not commanding
Rom. 12:3	It is being respectful, not looking down on.
1 Pet. 5:3	It is being exemplary, not domineering.
Rom. 12:10	It is being equal, not superior
Eph. 5:21	It is being mutually submissive, not coercive.

Leadership and management

Leadership and management are not the same. Leadership deals primarily with the broad picture of putting together a team and leading the team to do successful ministry. Management deals with the detailed work of actually making things happen. The gift of leadership fits the first category—the gift of administration the second.

The gift of faith

All Christians are admonished to have faith in God (Mark 11:22). We are also told that we are saved through faith that is itself a gift from God (Eph. 2:5). Beyond this, however, there is another kind of faith that is a direct gift of God to certain Christians.

Definition: *The gift of faith is the special ability that God gives to certain members of the body of Christ to discern with extraordinary confidence the will and purposes of God for His work.*

This kind of faith looks to the future rather than the past. People with this gift can see what God will do, even when it seems impossible. They are the inventors and promoters of plans, programs, and projects that would never become reality if this gift were not present. Peter Wagner writes: "They, like Noah, can obey God by building an ark on dry ground in the face of ridicule and criticism, having no doubt at all that God is going to send a flood."[5]

It is one of the leadership gifts in the sense that it sees how to move mountains when everyone else sees only impossibilities. People with this gift take risks and go out on a limb to accomplish things for the Kingdom of God, but they also use common sense and rational judgment. This kind of faith should not be confused with presumption. Presumption does things irrationally, basing its actions on feeling and misplaced perceptions of how God honors real faith.

Ellen White uses the example of Nehemiah to illustrate this kind of faith:

> The success attending Nehemiah's efforts shows what prayer, faith, and wise, energetic action will accomplish. Living faith will prompt to energetic action. The spirit manifested by the leader will be, to a great extent, reflected by the people.[6]

Some characteristics of people who have this gift are:

- An unusual desire to accept God's promises at face value and apply them until God fulfills them, just as He says He will.

- The recurring experience of sensing that God is going to do something unusual even though others do *not* have this kind of assurance.
- An attitude, in various crises that arise, not only that God *can* do something, but that He *will* do it.[7]

The gift of leadership

The gift of leadership involves inspiring people with a vision of what can be done—and setting the objectives and goals necessary to fulfill that vision.

Definition: *The gift of leadership is the special ability that God gives to certain members of the body of Christ to set goals in accordance with God's purposes for the future and to communicate these goals to others in such a way that they voluntarily and harmoniously work together to accomplish those goals for the glory of God.*

Intelligent leaders gain the good will of the people (Acts 7:10) and know how to bring divers elements together (Acts 15:13-21). Followers should respect leaders who are worthy of that respect (Heb. 13:17).

Leadership style

Leadership style is the way a person exercises leadership. Much of the success (or failure) of a leader has to do with leadership style. Is the leader kind and considerate—or dictatorial and demanding? Does he know how to talk kindly to people in a tone of voice that communicates consideration—or is he commanding and gruff? Efficiency is important, but getting the job done at the uncaring expense of people's feelings and capacities is counterproductive in the Christian world.

Ezra exercised a caring leadership style when he took three months to carefully go over records, interview people, and finally decide on those who were out of line (Ezra 10:16, 17). Dealing with the same issue, Nehemiah exercised an entirely different leadership style. In this case, he took the direct approach, which is sometimes necessary:

> I rebuked them and called curses down on them. I beat some of the men and pulled out their hair. I made them take an oath in God's name (Nehemiah 13:25).

Let's face it, it worked!

C. Peter Wagner sees the most effective role of the leader in the church as that of equipper:

> An equipper is a leader who actively sets goals for a congregation according to the will of God, obtains goal ownership from the people, and sees that each church member is properly motivated and equipped to do his or her part in accomplishing the goals.[8]

The gift of administration

The Greek word translated "administration" is *kubernesis*—the term for a ship's captain, the one who guides the ship to its destination. In modern Greece, the same word is applied to airline pilots. People with this gift are planners and goal setters. They are the ones who can organize a program or project and make it work. Leaders set the vision and inspire people to attain it. Administrators organize things so the vision can be attained. The KJV uses the word "governments" rather than administration, but that makes the gift sound more institutionalized than the Bible actually intends.

Definition: *The gift of administration is the special ability that God gives to certain members of the body of Christ to understand clearly the immediate and long-range goals of a particular unit of the body of Christ and to devise and execute effective plans for the accomplishment of those goals.*

Some biblical examples of the gift of administration would be: organizing the community services system in Jerusalem (Acts 6:1-8), planning to build a tower (Luke 4:28-30), and Paul's administrative assignment to Timothy (Titus 1:5).

People with this gift:

- Have abilities to organize things.

- Think in terms of helping others reach goals.
- Have a concern for the good of the entire group when in charge of the group.
- Don't mind managing or carrying out the details involved in initial planning done by others.

The gift of apostleship

The gift of apostleship is mentioned twice in the spiritual gifts lists: 1 Cor. 12:28 and Eph. 4:11. It is not the easiest gift to describe. Even in the early church there was discussion over just who were apostles. Everyone knows who the original twelve apostles were. The book of Acts uses the phrase "the apostles and the brothers" in distinguishing between the original twelve and other members (Acts 11:1), though it also identifies Paul and Barnabas as apostles (Acts 14:4). In Acts 15, the categorization becomes the "the apostles and the elders," since at some point the office of eldership was introduced. Paul mentions two of his relatives, Andronicus and Junias, and calls them apostles (Rom 16:7). He includes himself as an apostle, based on the revelation of Jesus he received on the road to Damascus (1 Cor. 9:5).

Some people masqueraded as apostles, but they were actually "false" apostles (2 Cor. 11:13). Some seemed to feel they were "super-apostles," apparently self-appointed (2 Cor. 12:11). The Greek term used for them in 2 Cor. 11:5 is one of disapprobation.[9]

Their behavior, according to 2 Cor. 11:20, left a lot to be desired. Paul described one of them as a person who "enslaves you or exploits you or takes advantage of you or pushes himself forward or slaps you in the face"—hardly the behavior one would expect from an apostle.

The Greek word *apostle* means "someone who is sent." This root meaning of the word has led some people to conclude that apostleship is the same as being a missionary or an evangelist, since both are sent to preach the gospel. Other people are of the opinion that apostleship was a special designation for the original twelve followers called by Jesus, or at least limited to those who were eyewitnesses to His ministry, plus Paul, who was called directly by Jesus to be an apostle.

Paul's ministry helps define the gift of apostleship

Careful study of Paul's ministry, however, gives us further insights on apostleship. Paul was a church planter. He went into unentered territory and started new churches. Later, he claimed certain authority because he was the founder of those churches (see 1 Cor. 9 and 2 Cor. 10). He was very careful, however, in how he used that authority (see 1 Cor. 9:12 and 2 Cor. 10:13-16). Two passages of Scripture outline how Paul both used and did not use the gift of apostleship—1 Cor. 9 and 2 Cor. 10. Careful study of these passages reveals an attitude of servant leadership and opposition to people who try to usurp the legitimate exercise of this gift.

The gift of apostleship today

Definition: *The gift of apostleship is the special ability that God gives to certain members of the body of Christ to assume and exercise general leadership over a number of churches, with an extraordinary authority in spiritual matters that is spontaneously recognized and appreciated by those churches.*

At first glance, this definition seems to describe the positions of elected officials usually termed church administrators. Based on Paul's experience as one of the first people to be considered an apostle outside the circle of the original twelve, however, and combined with the meaning of the term as "one sent," the definition above seems most applicable today to people who go into new areas, plant churches, and care for regional groups of churches when they are initially organized.

The original twelve apostles carry a special authority, because they were eyewitnesses to the ministry of Jesus and were the pioneers of the Christian church. While we know them through the pages of the New Testament as involved mostly with the affairs of the church in Jerusalem and the surrounding areas, church history presents some evidence that they actually went to the far corners of the globe establishing churches and spreading the gospel.[10] In this sense, they too were pioneers and church planters.

Those who have this gift often exhibit the following characteristics:

- A strong sense of a call by God for establishing new work.
- A forceful personality that trusts God to do what is necessary in unusual situations in order to establish authority for God's work.
- Usually an individual with multiple gifts that compliment the gift of apostle.
- A person who can sense what God wants to do and is not afraid to try.

Summary

Servant leadership is a system designed by God and exemplified in the Bible. The gifts of leadership, administration, and faith make servant leadership effective. These are the gifts that, in many ways, are the engine that drives the machinery of the church as she seeks to accomplish her mission of taking the message of the kingdom the world.

Notes:

1. Robert H. Pierson, *So You Want to Be a Leader* (Mountain View, Calif.: Pacific Press Publishing Association, 1966), 8.
2. Calvin B. Rock, *Church Leadership: A call to Virtue* (Boise, Idaho: Pacific Press Publishing Association, 1990).
3. Pierson, 9, 10.
4. C. Peter Wagner, *Leading Your Church to Growth*, (Ventura, Calif.: Regal Books, 1984) 115.
5. C. Peter Wagner, *Your Spiritual Gifts Can Help Your Church Grow*, revised edition (Ventura, Calif.: Regal Books, 1994), 146.
6. Ellen G. White, *Christian Service*, 177.

7. For additional information, read Heb. 11 and identify the people listed there who may have the gift of faith. See also Ellen White, *Steps to Christ*, 49-55. This chapter outlines a faith that all Christians should have. Notice, however, that those with the specific gift of faith have this attitude plus an extra measure of ability to put it into action. See also chapter 1 of Ellen White's book *Education* for an outline of the dynamics of human development as envisioned by the Lord.

8. C. Peter Wagner, *Leading Your Church to Growth* (Ventura, Calif.: Regal Books, 1984), 79.

9. *Seventh-day Adventist Bible Commentary*, 6:910.

10. There is no consensus on this point. See Kenneth Scott Latourette, *A History of the Expansion of Christianity,* 1: *"The First Five Centuries"* (Grand Rapids, Mich.: Zondervan Publishing Corporation, 1970), 101, for some information on this point. Look up the name of each apostle in a book such as J. D. Douglas (ed.) *The New International Dictionary of the Christian Church* (Grand Rapids, Mich.: Zondervan Publishing House, 1974) for additional information on where each may have gone.

NINE

Organizing Your Church for Action

A number of spiritual gifts fall under the classification of outreach gifts. They apply directly to the winning of converts. These gifts are often high-profile, and the people who have them tend to function in highly visible roles. In this chapter, we will consider the spiritual gifts of evangelism, tongues and interpretation of tongues, discernment, and missionary. It may seem strange that the gifts of tongues and interpretation of tongues are included in this classification, but the explanation that follows will clear up the reasons for including them.

Evangelism: Lifeblood of the church

Soul winning is the Lord's mandate for the church. No church can long survive if it is not winning converts. Ellen White points out that the Great Commission involves all Christians in every age who do the work of the Kingdom based on their spiritual gifts, embodies all races and classes, abolishes all national lines and prejudices, gathers believers into one church, is accompanied by signs and wonders as a confirmation of faith, possesses great power if requested by believers through faith, opens the doors to the inexhaustible supplies of heaven, and includes no laws ordained by ecclesiastical authority alone. If it is not carried out, the church becomes exclusive, the current of divine energy cannot flow, God is disappointed, the church invites spiritual feebleness and decay, love wanes, and faith grows dim.[1]

Utilizing the outreach gifts in a congregation makes soul-winning efficient and productive.

The Great Commission

The fundamental mandate of the Christian church is the Great Commission in Matt. 28:18-20. It presents a total plan, including growth in numbers, spiritual maturity, and the number of ministries carried out by a church. It is repeated four times in the Gospels, each time with a different emphasis (Matt. 28:16-20; Mark 16:14-20; Luke 24:44-47; John 20:21).

There are those who believe that the Great Commission applies only to the time of the early church. This was Martin Luther's view.[2] John Calvin used the Great Commission primarily to refute the Roman Catholic idea of apostolic succession and the Anabaptist rejection of infant baptism, adding only as an afterthought: "Christ wishes a mission of eternal salvation to be carried to all Gentiles."[3] When William Carey, the father of the modern missionary movement, mentioned his view of the continuing validity of the Great Commission at a minister's conference in the late 1790s, he was called a "miserable enthusiast." "When God pleases to convert the heathen," he was told, "he will do it without your aid or mine!"[4]

The Adventist view is that the Great Commission is valid for all time.[5] Ellen White wrote: "The very life of the church depends on her faithfulness in fulfilling the Lord's commission."[6] Though the Great Commission includes more than numbers of converts, it indicates that numerical growth is a paramount goal of the church. You can only disciple, baptize, and teach warm-blooded human beings. Ellen White's covering statement about the Great Commission is found in *The Desire of Ages*, 822:

> The Savior's commission to the disciples included all the believers. It includes all believers in Christ to the end of time. It is a fatal mistake to suppose that the work of saving souls depends alone on the

> ordained minister. All to whom the heavenly inspiration has come, are put in trust with the gospel. All who receive the life of Christ are ordained to work for the salvation of their fellow-men. For this work the church was established, and all who take upon themselves its sacred vows are thereby pledged to be co-workers with Christ.

What is evangelism?

Evangelism is the task of gaining converts, and the outreach gifts of the Spirit are designed to accomplish that task. The word *evangelism* comes from the Greek word *euongelizein*, a combination of two words, *eu*, meaning "good," and *angellein*, meaning "to carry news," or "to proclaim something." Also translated as "gospel," it appears 132 times in the New Testament. The word *euangelizo*, meaning "to evangelize," is used twenty-seven times, mostly by Luke and Paul. Luke uses it as a synonym for the proclamation of the good news. Paul uses it to explain the mission of Jesus, who came to bring "good news."

The word for an evangelist, *euangelistes*—a preacher of good news—occurs only three times, possibly because it was also a title of pagan priests, and the Bible writers were reluctant to use it. Philip (Acts 21:8) and Timothy (2 Tim. 4:5), are called *euangelistes*, and in Eph. 4:11 it identifies a specific spiritual gift.

The gift of evangelist

The gift of evangelism is unique. Those with this gift can lead people to decisions for the faith in ways that are almost impossible for others. The Lord gives them words to speak and places them in situations where they find receptive people.

Definition: *The gift of evangelism is the special ability that God gives to some members of the body of Christ to share the gospel with unbelievers in such a way that men and women become Jesus' disciples and responsible members of the body of Christ.*

An evangelist has a deep concern for the eternal well-being of people and for eternal issues. He or she is bold and confident when talking to others about the Lord. People with this gift are out on the front lines looking for converts. They are the people who like to knock on doors, engage people in conversations on buses and airplanes, visit people in their homes to give them Bible studies, and ask direct questions about people's willingness to accept the Lord.

Worldwide studies show that usually about 5 percent to 10 percent of a church's active membership may have the spiritual gift of evangelism. Why is this the case? The gift of evangelism is a specialized gift. Those having the gift develop skills in opening conversations, encouraging decisions, and doing the work of an evangelist (2 Tim. 4:5) with finesse and dexterity.

The silent 90 percent

If only around 10 percent of a congregation may have the gift of evangelism, what do the other 90 percent do? Are they then free of soul-winning responsibility? Not at all. The principle is this: *Not all Christians are evangelists, but all Christians* ***are*** *witnesses.*

Evangelism is a specialized, front-line, warrior-in-the-trenches gift. Witnessing is a skill all Christians must aquire. Anyone can tell what the Lord has done for him or her. Anyone can do a multitude of tasks that fit within the framework of discipleship and soul winning.

The importance of the gift of evangelism

The gift of evangelism is the primary means the Holy Spirit uses to reconcile men and women to God. It produces numeric growth and introduces people to the discipleship process. Some of the indications of this gift are:

- The ability to speak before large groups of people and converse easily with strangers and people of short acquaintance.
- The ability to persuade or influence people to accept the Lord.

- An intense spirit of unease at the thought of all the unsaved people in the world.
- The ability to insert spiritual truths into normal conversation with unsaved people—and the ability to sense the timing of when to do so.
- Freedom and joy in talking with people about Christian issues naturally and in an unforced manner.
- Unsaved people with whom you come in contact often end up making commitments to the Lord.

Types of evangelism

One of the difficulties we Seventh-day Adventists have with the gift of evangelism is our use of the word *evangelism* itself. To a Seventh-day Adventist, evangelism almost inevitably means "public meetings." There are, however, many kinds of evangelism. One author presents the following chart:[7]

Prayer Evangelism	Friendship Evangelism	Confrontation Evangelism	Teaching Evangelism	Public Evangelism	Follow-up Evangelism

Low-key .... High-key .... Decision

People with the spiritual gift of evangelism usually function best when involved at the confrontation - teaching - public-evangelism stages. Teaching evangelism, in this case, would include strategies such as seminar evangelism and small group Bible studies.

The gift of tongues

The gift of tongues is probably the most controversial of all the gifts, primarily because of the way it is so often misused and the erroneous theological presuppositions that have grown up around it. The practice had its biblical origin on the Day of Pentecost and became the center of attention in modern times—in North America at least—when a revival broke out at a small chapel on Azusa Street in Los Angeles around the turn of the century. Prior to that, Edward Irving's church in England experienced outbreaks of speaking in tongues.[8] Nineteenth-century Methodism experienced this phenomenon, as did early Adventism.[9]

What is the gift of tongues?

Based on Paul's statement in 1 Cor. 14:22—"Tongues, then, are a sign, not for believers but for unbelievers"—tongues might be classified as both an outreach gift and a sign gift. If Paul hadn't written what he did in 1 Cor. 14:13-18, the answer to the question "What is the gift of tongues?" would be easy—it is the ability to communicate the gospel in languages not one's own. The problem arises because Paul seems to be talking about some form of communication other than unlearned languages.

Those who understand the tongues in 1 Cor. 14 to be something other than unlearned languages see them as either a prayer language or a "heavenly" language.[10] The *Seventh-day Adventist Bible Commentary* presents arguments for both sides of the question.

Two recent Adventist books present opposite views on the issue. The late Gerhard Hassel took the position that tongues in the New Testament were a unique phenomenon unknown in other religions. "Tongues speaking in Corinth," he says, "is the miraculous speaking of unlearned foreign languages."[11] William E. Richardson takes the opposite position, affirming that the tongues phenomenon is not unique to Christianity, and that the tongues in 1 Cor. 14 were in fact given for private spiritual experience.[12]

Roland Hegstad examines both views and cites the conclusions of a special committee established by the General Conference in 1973 to study the charismatic movement. The committee offered suggestions on how church services should be run and outlined some of the consequences of disorderly conduct in worship, but made no statement about the nature of the gift of tongues in 1 Cor. 14. This ambivalence led Hegstad to entitle his chapter, "The Biblical Gift of Tongues Was_______" (you fill in the blank)[13]

The charismatic connection

Those of a Pentecostal persuasion usually interpret tongues as a sign to *believers* that they have been filled with the Holy Spirit. This is the exact opposite of Paul's statement in 1 Cor. 14:22. Kenneth Hagin, for instance, writes:

> Then as a sign or evidence that you have been filled [with the Holy Spirit], utterance in another tongue will be given to you. If you are simple enough in faith and strong enough in courage, you can speak that utterance out immediately.[14]

In an effort to prove that the gift of tongues is given to all Christians as proof of the baptism of the Holy Spirit, Hagin makes a division between ministry gifts and spiritual gifts. Ministry gifts, in his view, are the five gifts of apostle, teacher, evangelist, prophet, and pastor. These are authority gifts, exercised by clergy, or "the anointed." Lay members do not get these ministry gifts. This view is similar to the Roman Catholic view of the difference between clergy and laity.[15] Hagin's distinction between ministry and spiritual gifts is purely arbitrary and has no biblical basis.

We are still left, however, with Paul's injunctions: "I thank God that I speak in tongues more than all of you" and "do not forbid speaking in tongues." Whatever the gift was in the Corinthian church, it was an aberration of a true gift, though not very important in Paul's view (vs. 19), and, at least in this circumstance, a symptom of Christian immaturity (vs. 20). The most common manifestation of the gift of tongues, at least in most instances recorded in missionary history, is the ability to speak in languages not one's own because the circumstances demand it, and the Lord sees that this miraculous manifestation will convince someone of the validity of the gospel.

The gift of interpretation of tongues

The gift of interpretation of tongues is intimately related to the gift of tongues itself. When the gift of tongues is manifested publicly, it must be accompanied by interpretation, or it is useless.

Definition: *The gift of interpretation is the special ability that God gives to certain members of the body of Christ to make known in the vernacular the message of one who speaks in tongues.*

Interpretation is apparently more than translation from one language to another and is closer to a functional equivalent of the gift of prophecy. It is the ability to pass on a divinely inspired message in the vernacular so that people understand and get the point of the message.

The same enigma surrounds this gift as it does the gift of tongues. These gifts are not common, in spite of the anomalies witnessed in Pentecostal and charismatic circles. They remain components of a mixture of gifts designed to convince nonbelievers that the Spirit of God is present and functioning.

The gift of discernment

The gift of discernment is classified as an outreach gift, because it is part of the process of telling right from wrong in the presentation of the gospel. This gift is also called "discerning of spirits" (1 Cor. 12:10, KJV) and "distinguishing between spirits" (NIV). Others call it the gift of insight.

Definition: *The gift of discerning of spirits is the special ability God gives to some members of the body of Christ to know with assurance whether certain behavior purported to be of God is in reality divine, human, or satanic.*

First John 4:1 indicates that "spirits" have to be tested. In some ways, this could be classified as a sign or power gift, because the "spirits" discerned are often satanic. This is not a common gift and must be used judiciously. It also takes courage, and many people who have it are fearful of using it, because the consequences can be turbulent. In 1 Cor. 14:29, discussing the issue of orderliness in worship services, Paul counsels, "Two or three prophets should speak, and the others should *weigh carefully* what is said." The words "weigh carefully" (NIV) or "let the other judge" (KJV) are the same Greek words translated "discernment" in other texts.

Some characteristics of those who have this gift are:

- A keen ability to recognize inconsistencies.
- The tendency to spot what is wrong with an idea or teaching and to suggest how to fix it.
- A deep conviction not easily put to rest when those with the gift know that people are being given half-truths, misapplied truth, or false teachings—and are being asked to act on these erroneous teachings.

H.M.S. Richards, the founder of the Voice of Prophecy radio program, was a well-known opponent of the Mormon church. He used to tell us the story of the time he was pitching a tent in a certain city and a man came up to him and began discussing religion. It was obvious that the man knew who Elder Richards was, but Elder Richards didn't know him. It was also obvious that he was opposed to the message Richards was about to present in the upcoming meetings. Suddenly, in the midst of the conversation, the man stopped and said, "Do you know who I am?" Elder Richards related that in a flash the answer was given him. "Yes," he said, "You're bishop so-and-so of the Mormon church, and you've been sent here especially to oppose these meetings." The man was astounded. "How did you know that?" he asked. Elder Richards told us he just couldn't resist the opportunity of the moment. "Oh," he said, "I've got discerning of spirits!" It so frightened the Mormon bishop that he never did show up to oppose the meetings. While Elder Richards never claimed the gift of discerning of spirits as a life-long ministry—and told us the story as an anecdote—at that moment the Lord really gave him that gift as a witness to unbelievers of His presence and power.

The gift of missionary

The gift of missionary is not mentioned directly in the Scriptures, but is alluded to in Rom. 1:5: "Through him and for his name's sake, we received grace and apostleship to call people from among all the Gentiles to the obedience that comes from faith." It refers to the ability to work cross-culturally. Not everyone can do this, nor are all called to do so.

Definition: *The gift of missionary is the special ability that*

God gives to some members of the body of Christ to minister whatever other spiritual gifts they have in a second culture.

There are different types of outreach, usually classified according to the target group the evangelizers wish to reach:

- The internal spiritual growth of an existing congregation.
- Bringing new converts from the community into an existing congregation.
- Planting new churches.
- Reaching out to people groups of a different ethnicity, language, or cultural background.

People with the gift of missionary may work at any of these points, though most often they function at point four, and often serve outside their country of origin.

Paul is an example of someone with this gift. In outlining his personal gifts, he says he was sent to all nations (Rom. 1:5), called to minister especially to Gentiles (Rom. 15:16; Gal. 2:7, 8), and to be a teacher of Gentiles (1 Tim. 2:7). To take the gospel to the Gentiles was so unheard of in Paul's time that to the end of his life, he still marveled that it had happened. He called it a mystery that they could be grafted into the Hebrew tree (Rom. 11:25). Peter, on the other hand, did not have the gift of missionary. On occasion he preached to non-Jews, but his assigned ministry was to his own people (Gal. 2:7, 8).

Care needs to be taken in distinguishing between the lack of the gift of missionary and racial or ethnic prejudice and lack of brotherly love. The lack of the gift of missionary does not excuse anyone from loving their fellow human beings. Spiritual gifts are operational tools designed to accomplish assigned tasks for the advancement of the Kingdom of God. These gifts must always be encased in love to be effective. All Christians are called to love one another. Certain ones are called to cross-cultural tasks and to dedicate their lives to multi-cultural ministry. Let's don't confuse the two and allow the spirit of the world to produce ethnic or cultural attitudes that are both wrong and counterproductive to the advancement of the kingdom.

Summary

The outreach gifts are the frontline gifts used by the Holy Spirit to make initial inroads into the Devil's territory and to convince people of the truth. They are indispensable to the work of the church and should be the object of continually increasing skill and employment.

Notes:

1. See *The Desire of Ages*, 818-828.
2. T. F. Torrance, *Les Reformateurs et la Fin des Temps* (Paris: Delachaux & Niestles, S. A. 1955).
3. David B. Calhoun, "John Calvin: Missionary Hero or Missionary Failure?" *Presbyterion,* No. 1, (Spring), 16-33.
4. Harold R. Cook, *Highlights of Christian Missions* (Chicago: Moody Press, 1967), 55.
5. See Fundamental Belief No. 11, *Seventh-day Adventist Church Manual.*
6. Ellen G. White, *The Desire of Ages*, 825.
7. Bobby Clinton, *Spiritual Gifts* (Beaverlodge, Alberta, Canada: Horizon House Publishers, 1985), p. 151.
8. For the history of this movement, see Arnold Dallimore, *Forerunner of the Charismatic Movement* (Chicago: Moody Press, 1983), and LeRoy E. Froom, *Prophetic Faith of Our Fathers* (Washington, D.C.: Review and Herald Publishing Association, 1946), 3:514-532.
9. For insights into charismatic experiences in Adventism, see Roland R. Hegstad, *Rattling the Gates* (Washington, D.C.: Review and Herald Publishing Association, 1974), 101-133.
10. Nicholas Fisher, *Understanding Tongues* (Lincolnshire, England: Stanborough Press, nd.)
11. Gerhard F. Hassel, *Speaking in Tongues* (Berrien Springs, Mich.: Andrews University Press, 1991), 143.

12. William E. Richardson, *Speaking in Tongues* (Hagerstown, Md.: Review and Herald Publishing Association, 1994), 92.
13. Roland R. Hegstad, *Rattling the Gates* (Washington, D.C.: Review and Herald Publishing Association, 1974), 53-77.
14. Kenneth E. Hagin, *The Holy Spirit and His Gifts* (Tulsa, Okla.: RHEMA Bible Church, 1991), 42.
15. For information on what the priesthood of all believers really means, see Rex D. Edwards, *Every Believer a Minister* (Washington, D.C.: General Conference Ministerial Association, 1995).

TEN

Signs and Wonders, Power and Glory

The phrase "signs and wonders" first appears in a letter from Nebuchadnezzar, King of Babylon, to his subjects (Dan. 4) and reappears in Peter's sermon on the day of Pentecost (Acts 2:22). The purpose of signs and wonders is to confirm to unbelievers and skeptical believers that God is indeed working in a marked way in a particular circumstance. The specific spiritual gifts closely related to signs and wonders are miracles, prophecy, healings, deliverance, intercession, martyrdom, voluntary poverty, and celibacy.

Biblical perspectives on signs and wonders

The Greek word for miracles, *dunamis*, means inherent power, the power residing in something by virtue of its nature, or the power a person or thing exerts and puts forth. Wonders, *terata* in Greek, indicate the effect of the *dunamis* on the observers, almost always astonishment. Signs, *semeia* in Greek, refer to seals or verifications God uses to authenticate the persons by whom the miracles and wonders are wrought.[1] Thus Jesus' disciples affirmed: "This salvation, which was first announced by the Lord, was confirmed to us by those who heard him. God also testified to it by signs, wonders and various miracles, and gifts of the Holy Spirit distributed according to his will" (Hebrews 2:4).

Do signs and wonders really happen?

Signs and wonders are often so sensational and highly publicized that they frighten people, especially in the scientifically oriented Western world. Two things lend themselves to these perceptions. First, it's relatively easy to acknowledge signs and wonders as long as they happen at a physical distance from us personally. When they happen close to home, it's typical to be skeptical and reticent to acknowledge their validity.

Second, its an almost spontaneous reaction to downplay miracles, signs, and wonders, because they can easily be confused with counterfeits. Paul himself warned: "The coming of the lawless one will be in accordance with the work of Satan displayed in all kinds of counterfeit miracles, signs and wonders, and in every sort of evil that deceives those who are perishing" (2 Thess. 2:9, 10). The existence of counterfeits, however, does not nullify the validity of the genuine.

"With signs following"

Miracles, signs, and wonders comprise a broad spectrum of events and activities promised to Jesus' followers in Mark's version of the Great Commission:

> And these signs will accompany those who believe: In my name they will drive out demons; they will speak in new tongues; they will pick up snakes with their hands; and when they drink deadly poison, it will not hurt them at all; they will place their hands on sick people, and they will get well (Mark 16:15-18).[7]

Ellen White affirms that this promise is still alive and well on Planet Earth:

> As, like the disciples, you go from place to place, telling the story of the Savior's love. . . . The sick will be ministered to, the afflicted prayed for. There will be heard the voice of singing and the voice of prayer. The Scriptures will be opened to testify of

> truth. And with signs following, the Lord will confirm the word spoken.—*Advent Review and Sabbath Herald*, Feb. 4, 1904.

Power encounters

These phenomena are called "power" gifts, because they often appear at times when believers find it necessary to go face to face with the forces of evil and demonstrate visibly and dramatically who is the more powerful—God or Satan. This kind of confrontation is known as a "power encounter." The classic Old Testament example is Elijah's encounter with the prophets of Baal on Mt. Carmel (1 Kings 18). Others include Jesus' confrontation with a legion of demons in the cemetery in Gadara (Mark 5) and Paul's showdown with Elymas the sorcerer (Acts 13:6-12).

A review of the skirmishes between Nebuchadnezzar and Daniel illustrates how these power encounters work. When Nebuchadnezzar, renowned king of Babylon, wrote the following to his subjects, he was talking from personal experience:

> It is my pleasure to tell you about the miraculous signs and wonders that the Most High God has performed for me. How great are his signs, how mighty his wonders! His kingdom is an eternal kingdom; his dominion endures from generation to generation (Daniel 4:2, 3).

Nebuchadnezzar was an absolute monarch with the power of life and death in his hands, the ruler of the known world, and a proponent of the law of an eye for an eye and a tooth for a tooth built into the Babylonian law code designed by his predecessor Hammurabi. Nebuchadnezzar had no national assembly to question his commands, wishes or desires—no checks and balances on anything he did.[3] An accomplished builder, he could truthfully say (though too arrogantly) "Is not this the great Babylon I have built as the royal residence, by my mighty power and for the glory of my majesty?" (Daniel 4:30).

Behind all this pomp and circumstance, however, lay a series of encounters that eventually led Nebuchadnezzar to acknowledge a Power greater than himself. Again and again that Power beat him at his own game. Vegetarians from a conquered land became his main advisors, dreams were interpreted and came true to the letter, uncompromising servants of the God of Israel wouldn't burn in the hottest of flames, and Daniel himself informed the king of a coming bout with madness. It took only one heavenly messenger, or "watcher" as the KJV puts it, to fulfill that prediction and reduce Nebuchadnezzar to the status of a cow! Signs and wonders became the evidence he needed to cross the line and take a stand on the side of the God of Heaven.[4]

Power or sign gifts

Power or sign gifts come into play when it is necessary to convince someone that the God of heaven is superior to any other proposed god, or to the powers of evil—and to give specific instruction to God's people. They are evidences to unbelievers and skeptical believers that God is indeed working in a certain circumstance or occasion. John Calvin wrote:

> Paul calls them *signs*, because they are not empty shows, but are appointed for the instruction of mankind; *wonders*, because they ought, by their novelty, to arouse men and strike them with astonishment; and *mighty deeds*, because they are more signal tokens of divine power than what we behold in the ordinary course of nature.[5]

Not frequent manifestations

These power gifts, however, appear infrequently. Prophetic utterances, for instance, may be impressive phenomena, often accompanied by unique physical manifestations, but full-time prophets are few and far between. There are only about fifty prophets mentioned in the entire time span of biblical history. Healings through the use of scientific medicine are far more frequent than miraculous healings. There are, nevertheless, spiritually gifted people who pray for others, following the principles laid down in the book of James, and people get well. There are people who pray for miracles, and miracles happen.

Do miracles still happen?

Do these things happen today, or are they confined to ancient historical records and missionary stories from too far away for verification? Are they usually just counterfeits, playing tricks with the autonomic nervous system?

Counterfeits are always around. There are quacks, charlatans, and sensationalist faith healers. They blow on people and supposedly cause them to be slain in the Spirit, hit people on the head and ask if they see lights (who wouldn't?), and call these actions the "wonders" referred to in the Bible.

Counterfeits, however, don't negate the genuine. They make us cautious, but not so cautious that we turn off the power of God. As C. S Lewis observes:

> God does not shake miracles into Nature at random. . . . they come on great occasions; they are found at the great ganglions of history. . . . If your life does not happen to be near one of those great ganglions, how should you expect to see one?[6]

Signs and wonders are part of a larger picture we call the "great controversy"—the entire picture of eschatology from the time of Jesus until the second coming. Within that time span, the Lord works through the power of the Holy Spirit to unchain human minds and reorient them toward the kingdom of God. Jesus "disarmed the powers and authorities [and] made a public spectacle of them, triumphing over them at the cross" (Col. 2:15).

That victory, however, while final in the long run, was not the end of the war. Satan continues to blind people's spiritual eyes (2 Cor. 4:4); block spiritual discernment (1 Cor. 2:14); cause them to see evil as good (Rom. 1:24); and distort spiritual discernment with false doctrines (Rev. 14:8). Most of the time, solid biblical teaching in the form of Bible studies, classes, study groups, and sermons is the vehicle by which these conditions are reversed (Rom. 10:17). When circumstances call for it, however, the Lord works through His people in marked, visible manifestations that we call signs and wonders.[7]

The gift of miracles

Definition: *The gift of miracles is the special ability that God gives to certain members of the body of Christ to serve as human intermediaries, through whom it pleases God to perform powerful acts that are perceived by observers to have altered the ordinary.*

The Bible is filled with stories of the miraculous.[8] Children are born to barren parents, vast numbers of people cross bodies of water that dry up before their eyes, a huge fish swallows a reluctant prophet and later regurgitates him at a designated geographical location. The blind see, people with incurable disease are healed, thousands are fed from a small boy's lunch pail, and even the dead live again.

The early church understood miracles to verify the validity of the message they taught (Acts 2:22), and the resurrection of Jesus, an astounding miracle verified by both believers and nonbelievers, became the centerpiece of apostolic preaching (Acts 17:31).

Missionary history and contemporary church life are also replete with stories of miracles.

A general category

"Miracles" is a general category for the kinds of signs and wonders we have considered so far. The basic purpose of miracles is to awaken and strengthen faith in God. "They focus attention on the real source of all that is good in the world; they remind us that God is indeed alive and well."[9]

The gift of healing

Definition: *The gift of healing is the special ability that God gives to certain members of the body of Christ to serve as human intermediaries, through whom it pleases God to cure* *illnesses and restore health apart from the use of natural means.*

Divine healing, usually as a direct answer to prayer, is often mentioned in Scripture and religious literature. The following story illustrates the point. A thirty-year-old woman diagnosed with colon cancer was told she only had two months to live. She was prayed for and anointed on a Sabbath afternoon. Three days later, her doctor, an atheist, told her, "You must serve a very powerful God!" because he could find no trace of the cancer.[10]

The sensationalist character of the activities of self-styled faith healers, witch doctors, shamans, etc., does not discount the validity of miraculous healings through prayer. The popularity of these aberrations, however, makes instances of the true gift of miraculous healing less frequent.

The Bible uses the plural, "healings," (1 Cor. 12:28), possibly refers to the application of the gift to different kinds of diseases, such as emotional and spiritual illnesses, as well as physical healing. The gift of healing does not give a person supernatural power over diseases. It doesn't make doctors and nurses obsolete, nor are healings always permanent. As far as we know, even the people Jesus healed eventually died. Paul had a "thorn in the flesh" (2 Cor. 12:7-9) that the Lord chose not to heal. Paul recommended a natural remedy for Timothy's stomach problem rather than handing him a "sacred handkerchief," used with great effect in Ephesus (Acts 19:12).

Following this lead, Ellen White often connects this gift with medical missionary work.

> God's miracles do not always bear the outward semblance of miracles. Often they are brought about in a way which looks like the natural course of events. When we pray for the sick, we also work for them. We answer our own prayers by using the remedies within our reach.[11]

In summary, the Scripture does not specifically define how God handles disease and illness, and those assigned the gift of healing do not manipulate God. They are simply instruments in His hands to be used in the time and place He sees fit.

The gift of prophecy

Definition: *The gift of prophecy is the special ability that God gives to certain members of the body of Christ to receive and communicate an immediate message from God to His people through a divinely appointed utterance.*

The gift of prophecy is well known among Seventh-day Adventists. It is a sign or power gift in the sense that (1) it is not very common, and (2) it is a specific indication that God is working in a direct way in a particular circumstance. The gift may be long-term, which we believe to be the case for Ellen White, or it may be short-term, given to help in a particular circumstance or issue.

Prophecy and authority

The primary problem with the gift of prophecy is the matter of authority. No prophetic utterance today can supersede the authority of the canon of Scripture. Self-proclamation as a "prophet" does not make one so. Any prophetic utterance must first of all be tested by the Scripture before it can be accepted (1 Thess. 5:19-21). Most prophecy is not predictive—it is instruction from God to His people, often called "classical" prophecy. This is one reason Ellen White consistently termed herself a "messenger" rather than a prophetess.[12]

The gift of prophecy is sometimes linked to preaching. This, however, is not always the case. Preaching may be "prophetic" in the sense that it expounds the Word of God, but it is the Word of God, the Scriptures, that contain the prophetic element, not the preaching itself.

The gift of deliverance or exorcism

Definition: *The gift of deliverance (or exorcism) is the special ability that God gives to certain members of the body of Christ to cast out demons and evil spirits.* (Matt. 12:22-32; Luke 10:17-20; Acts 8:5-8).

Casting out devils is a form of power encounter, and certain people receive this spiritual gift. On the one hand, few spiritual gifts are as spectacular as this one. In the Bible there are numerous stories of deliverance. Some contemporary people, however, who claim to have this gift assign "devils" to every malady of human nature, from headaches to family infighting. This view has little biblical evidence to support it.

On the other hand, the closer we approach the second coming, and God's Spirit is withdrawn from the earth, the more opportunity Satan has to work openly. If this gift is not used judiciously and under careful control, however, it can easily be counterfeited by Satan himself and turned into an apparent victory for him rather than for the Lord (See Mark 9:14-29).[13]

The gift of intercession

Definition: *The gift of intercession is the special ability that God gives to certain members of the body of Christ to pray for extended periods of time on a regular basis and see frequent answers to their prayers—to a degree much greater than that expected of the average Christian.* (James 5:14-16; 1 Tim. 2:1, 2; Col. 4:12, 13.)

Intercessory prayer is a type of prayer focused on a particular issue. Experience demonstrates that every church has someone with this gift. It is one of the most powerful gifts a church can have. An intercessory prayer ministry in your church will produce miracles, both spectacular and "quiet," in astounding ways. It will transform the ministry and growth of your church.[14]

Three unusual gifts

Martyrdom, voluntary poverty, and celibacy are alluded to as spiritual gifts in the New Testament (1 Cor. 13). These would seem to be very unusual "power gifts." When you think about them, though, they make sense.

The gift of martyrdom.

Definition: *The gift of martyrdom is the special ability that God gives to some members of the body of Christ to undergo* *suffering for the faith, even to death, while consistently displaying a joyous and victorious attitude that brings glory to God.*

History tells us that martyrs, surprisingly, face death for the cause of the Lord with a unique attitude. They go down singing, praising God, and giving highly visible testimony to their dedication.[15]

The gift of voluntary poverty

Definition: *The gift of voluntary poverty is the special ability that God gives to some members of the body of Christ to renounce material comfort and luxury and adopt a personal lifestyle equivalent to those living at the poverty level in a given society, in order to serve God more effectively.*

Some Christians have chosen to live at the poverty level in order to minister to others at the same level. Mother Teresa is a modern-day example. Teams of people in cities around the world have made this choice, and they do very well, due to the Lord's blessing. Their decisions and lifestyles are a living example to unbelievers of dedication and selflessness for the cause of the Kingdom—and wins converts. In this sense, this is a sign to unbelievers that the Lord is truly working through these disciples.

The gift of celibacy

Definition: *The gift of celibacy is the special ability that God gives to some members of the body of Christ to remain single and enjoy it—to be unmarried and not suffer undue sexual temptations.*

The gift of celibacy is not the same as being single. A person with this gift consciously decides to remain single in order to dedicate time and energy to the Lord's work that might otherwise go into family affairs. The fact that they do this is a testimony or sign to unbelievers of their dedication. When I first heard about this gift, I thought it was pushing the point a little. The only example I knew of would be Paul himself (1 Cor. 7). Frankly, most people I've known who were single were not really all that happy about it, and some were definitely not having an easy time as far as sexual activity was concerned. But in the course of leading out in spiritual gifts seminars, I did discover people with this gift who confirmed that it was true. So, though it may be unusual and rare, it is a definite spiritual gift.

Summary

Power or sign gifts usually function to resolve extraordinary problems—or as evidence to unbelievers of the power of God. Some gifts in this category, such as celibacy and voluntary poverty, are low-key, but still signs of the power of God manifest in unusual ways. The gift of prophecy is normally a lifelong assignment, though it may be temporarily assigned to deal with a particular circumstance.

Due to their often spectacular character, sign or power gifts must be verified and used judiciously. This fact, however, should not be allowed to discount their appearance and application in the life of the church.

Notes:

1. H. Orton Wiley, *Christian Theology* (Kansas City: Beacon Hill Press, 1950), 1:151.
2. There is some question about the authenticity of these verses. See Donald Guthrie, *New Testament Introduction*, revised edition (Downer's Grove, Ill.: InterVarsity Press, 1990), 89-93, for a summary of the debate. The *Seventh-day Adventist Bible Commentary* is of the opinion that textual evidence favors the inclusion of these verses (5:658). Ellen White cites these verses as authoritative scripture (*The Kress Collection*, 126).
3. For an interesting survey of Nebuchadnezzar, his kingdom, and his system of laws, see Will Durante, *Our Oriental Heritage* (New York: Simon and Schuster, 1954), 218-264. Durante considers the book of Daniel to be mythology, but his historical data is worth reading.
4. "King Nebuchadnezzar, before whom Daniel so often honored

the name of God, was finally thoroughly converted, and learned to 'praise and extol and honor the King of heaven'"—Ellen White, *Review and Herald*, Jan. 11, 1906.

5. Quoted in R.V.G. Tasker, *The Second Epistle of Paul to the Corinthians* (Grand Rapids,Mich.: Wm. B. Eerdmans Publishing Company, 1958), 180.

6. C. S. Lewis, *Miracles: A Preliminary Study* (New York: The Macmillian Company, 1947), 167, 168.

7. For a contemporary evaluation of spiritual warfare and the various points of view involved, see Thomas H. McAlpine, *Facing the Powers* (Monrovia, Calif.: MARC, 1991) and John White, *When the Spirit Comes With Power* (Downers Grove, Ill.: InterVarsity Press, 1988). For two theological analyses, see Merrill F. Unger, *Demons in the World Today* (Wheaton, Ill.: Tyndale House Publishers, Inc., 1971) and Donald Grey Barnhouse, *The Invisible War* (Grand Rapids, Mich.: Zondervan Publishing House, 1965). For a cautious evaluation, see Thomas Ice and Robert Dean. Jr, *Overrun by Demons* (Eugene, Ore.: Harvest House Publishers, 1990). See Ed Murthy, *The Handbook of Spiritual Warfare* (Nashville: Thomas Nelson Publishers, 1992) for an encyclopedic source of information.

8. C.S. Lewis, *Miracles: A Preliminary Study* (New York: The Macmillan Company, 1960) is a good general treatise on miracles.

9. Richard Rice, *The Reign of God* (Berrien Springs, Mich.: Andrews University Press, 1985), 83.

10. Reported by Rich DuBose in *FYE*, the North American Division information newsletter, Dec. 11, 1995.

11. Ellen White comments, *S.D.A. Bible Commentary,* 7:938.

12. Ellen White, *Selected Messages*, 1:32.

13. For more information on devil possession and the gift of exorcism, see *Seventh-day Adventist Bible Commentary*, 5:575-578 and *The Great Controversy*, chapter 31. There have been outbreaks of so-called "deliverance ministries" in the Adventist church that have gone far beyond the bounds of

biblical guidelines. For more information, you can obtain a number of documents from the General Conference Biblical Research Institute on this subject.

14. For more information on intercessory prayer, see Dorothy Eaton Watts, *Prayer Country* (Boise, Idaho: Pacific Press Publishing Association, 1993); C.E. Bradford, *Find Out About Prayer* (Fallbrook, Calif.: Hart Research Center, 1993); Kurt Johnson, *Prayer Works* (Fallbrook, Calif.: Hart Research Center, 1993). Johnson's book is designed for use in small groups.
    C. Peter Wagner, *Churches That Pray* (Ventura, Calif.: Regal Books, 1993) presents a concept called "action prayer" that has renewed many churches.

15. For an account of present-day martyrs, see James and Marti Hefely, *By Their Blood: Christian Martyrs of the 20th Century* (Milford, Mich.: Mott Media, 1979).

ELEVEN

Unwrapping Your Spiritual Gifts

In 1948, five friends, all businessmen, felt—along with their families—a need for a warmer time of fellowship than they were getting in their respective churches. They rented a small room in the local Community Center and began meeting together on Sunday evenings for informal fellowship and Bible teaching. None of them knew the meaning of the Greek word *koinonia* (fellowship), but that's what they were seeking.

The news got around through word of mouth about this small group, and others began to attend. A year or so later, about one hundred people were showing up regularly. Some of the people asked if they couldn't also meet in the morning, since their children needed the kind of Bible teaching going on in the evening. By 1950, a church was born and the first pastor called.

All this time, the leaders—church members with no theological training—knew nothing about spiritual gifts or biblical principles of church organization. They only knew that what was happening was blessing their lives and was attracting a lot of people. They had no spectacular services. They weren't charismatic. They had no healing meetings or spectacular "slain in the Spirit" manifestations. They just studied from the Bible and fellowshiped, meeting human needs as best they could and "bearing one another's burdens."

The pastor they called recounts that he had one deep conviction, derived from his personal study of Ephesians 4—that ministry belongs to the people, not to the pastor. Initially, he didn't know how to implement that conviction—or even how to teach the principle to the members. He knew only that he had learned this from his Bible study.

We'll come back to that church in a minute.

Evangelizing the evangelized

Most churches, soon after they start, end up evangelizing the evangelized and preaching to the choir! Few new people appear, and when they do, they are often Christians who have moved into the area and are looking for a church. Too often, as we saw in the first chapter of this book, people assume that ministry is the work of the pastor.

Many people, including pastors, feel that the church is a waiting room, waiting for the next bus that will take them to heaven! So saints "congregate" once a week to sing a little, pray a little, enjoy a sermon which is hopefully enjoyable, and drop back into daily existence until the next "congregation" a week away.

Back to our church

The new church we were talking about made a unique decision. It decided that it would do no direct evangelizing, meaning it would hold no public campaigns or even make altar calls, within the church building. (Be patient. To build a case for a concept, I'm simply describing what one church did.) This church decided that all evangelizing would be done in homes, back yards, rented halls, or other public places. Who did all this outreach? Church members who were taught how to discover and use their spiritual gifts. "These home meetings," the pastor later wrote, "were regarded as the personal ministry of the Christians involved."[1]

Who ran the internal affairs of the church? The members organized themselves along New Testament lines, and the pastor dedicated himself primarily to unfolding the Word of

God. Members did visitation, took care of the church finances, and presided at church services.

This church went on to become not only large, but a training center for members, interns, theology students in training, and others who wanted to learn how to do the same in their churches.

Keys to success

What were the keys to success in this church? First, it organized itself around the principles described in the New Testament. Second, the members were trained to identify and use their spiritual gifts. Third, the church developed down-to-earth ministries around the principle of *koinonia* that helped thousand of people and at the same time taught them the meaning of the gospel.

Unwrapping your spiritual gifts

How do you go about unwrapping your spiritual gifts? First, let's review what we have learned so far. Spiritual gifts are assigned by the Holy Spirit to all Christians as part of the new- birth process. They are designed to function as tools for the building up of the Kingdom of God. They may or may not match natural talents. Whether they do or not depends on what the Holy Spirit has in mind. No gift is superior or inferior to any other.

The application of all gifts will build a sense of unity into the church, focusing its energies on the primary job of winning converts for the kingdom and preparing them for the earth made new. Spiritual gifts empower immediately, but still need to be developed. Once a person knows what his gifts are, he is responsible for the lifelong development of those gifts.

For instance, in the church we've used as an example, two of the original five founders developed their spiritual gifts so well that a few years later, responding to the call of the Lord, they became associate pastors of the church, dedicating their full time to the ministries they had developed as church members.

A four-stage process

Spiritual gifts are unwrapped in a four-stage process:

1. Discover your most probable gifts through your own inward convictions and the use of a spiritual gifts inventory.

2. Ask the Lord to confirm your gifts through intercessory prayer (James 1:5).

3. Have the church body verify the findings of the inventory.

4. Use your gifts in ministry.

Let's go through this process step by step.

Step 1: What gifts do you have?

Experience in the Christian life, and service to the church, have already unveiled some things about your spiritual gifts. You may not have thought of it in the same way as we have outlined it in this book, but you may already be exercising your gifts. Two principles are important. First, a restless, growing conviction is often the first sign that God has endowed you with a combination of gifts necessary to meet a need in the church. Second, a specific call by the Lord to a ministry will inevitably be accompanied by the gifts that will make that ministry effective, provided that a person's motivation and attitude follow biblical guidelines and principles.

An inward-conviction questionnaire

Fill out the following inward-conviction questionnaire.

1. I have a growing conviction and restlessness in my heart that tells me I ought to be doing the following in the church:
   a. I should get involved in ____________________.
   b. I know about a special need that I could fill. (Describe that need.)
   c. Which of the spiritual gifts best relate to this conviction you have?
2. I am certain that God has called me to a specific ministry. (Describe that ministry.)

3. What gifts are necessary for that ministry—and do I feel I have them?
4. Do I truly feel that God could develop these gifts in me, and is it important for the church that He do so?
5. Am I willing to actively and consistently carry out that ministry with conviction and expertise?
6. Of all the Christians I know, the ministry of which two of them has impressed me the most?
   a. What gifts do these two have?
   b. Are those the same gifts I feel I have—and do I believe I could accomplish a ministry similar to theirs?

Experience demonstrates that spiritual gifts often come in cognate pairs. A primary gift is combined with another gift that makes the primary one more useful and functional. Sometimes people with a high-profile gift will want to form a team or component with people who have cognate gifts. For instance, notice in the following chart how cognate gifts help accomplish various types of evangelism:

TYPE OF EVANGELISM	COGNATE GIFT(S)	CHURCH INVOLVEMENT
Prayer Evangelism	Intercessory prayer	All Christians can witness at these stages.
Friendship Evangelism	Exhortation / encouragement	
Confrontation Evangelism	Discernment of spirits	The gift of evangelism is essential here.
Public Evangelism	Faith	
Confirmation Evangelism	Teaching	The entire congregation may be involved.

A spiritual gifts inventory

Spiritual-gifts inventories take you through descriptions of spiritual gifts in action and ask if you have experienced these events, feelings, convictions, or actions in your life. You can then identify your three or four most prominent gifts and some secondary ones. These inventories are only a start in the process of identifying spiritual gifts, but they are valuable as initial tools in the process.

The Seventh-day Adventist Church produces an excellent series of study materials on spiritual gifts authored by Dr. Roy Naden, entitled *Your Spiritual Gifts: Making the Great Discovery*.[2] The set includes videos, an instruction book, and a spiritual-gifts inventory. This series helps you identify five clusters of gifts; teacher cluster, shepherd/evangelist cluster, support cluster, counselor cluster, and leader cluster. This inventory does not cover the power or sign gifts, taking the position that they are self-evident.

A spiritual gifts inventory called the *Wagner-Modified Houts Questionnaire* is available from many Adventist Book Centers, conference departments, and Christian bookstores. It is also is found in C. Peter Wagner's, *Your Spiritual Gifts Can Help Your Church Grow*.[3] Originally developed by a Dr. Richard F. Houts, this questionnaire contains 125 statements that cover all the gifts mentioned in this book. It was modified by Peter Wagner to match the format and organization of his book. Some of the statements in this questionnaire sound strange to Adventist ears, but it is still a useful tool for identifying your spiritual gifts.

Step 2: Intercessory prayer and confirmation by the Lord

The second step in the process is to receive confirmation from the Lord. You may not hear an audible voice from heaven confirming your gifts, but the Lord will let you know in His own way. Asking people with the gift of intercessory prayer to pray with and for you for confirmation will bring an answer and an assurance that you are finding the Lord's will.

Step 3: Confirmation by the church body

The third step is confirmation by the body of the church. A biblical example is that of Paul, Barnabas, and the church in Antioch. Acts 13:1-3 says the church fasted and prayed, laid hands on them, and sent them off to the mission field. This happened after the Holy Spirit had clearly endowed them with the gift of missionary, among others. Timothy's experience was identical. His gift, the Scripture states, was given through a prophetic message when the body of elders laid their hands on him (1 Tim. 4:14).

If a church congregation knows nothing about spiritual gifts, or has no idea how to confirm these gifts in other people, talk to friends and people you work with in the church. They will affirm your gifts. Experience shows that even if an inventory reveals gifts that may surprise you, the people who know you will probably say "we knew that all the time."

Step 4: Use your gift

Spiritual gifts are given to be used. Often there are skills to be learned that make the gifts more effective. For instance, if you have the gift of teaching, then in the church, you will be teaching the Bible. That means you need to develop the skills of Bible study and interpretation, as well as methods of Bible teaching. (See chart on following page.)

Spiritual gifts can be abused

Spiritual gifts can be abused in a number of ways. The most common abuse is to identify one's gift and then say something like, "Well, that's it. Unless they give me such and such an office or position, I won't do anything!" Or to say. "Good, since I don't have the gift of . . . , I don't have to participate in . . . any more." As we noted in chapter 1, spiritual gifts are assignments of a lifelong, primary ministry or ministries. That doesn't preclude fulfilling tasks that have to be done. The difference is that tasks are short-term and based on current needs. Ministries based on spiritual giftedness are long-term. Spiritual giftedness implies expertise, continuing education,

STEP	PROCEDURE	FOLLOW-UP SUGGESTIONS
1	Make certain you have a clear understanding of the basic principles of biblical interpretation	■ Master the skill of biblical interpretation so you know how to interpret biblical information ■ You may teach at different age levels, but the principles of biblical interpretation are the same.
2	Develop a system of Bible study that will continually increase your knowledge. You can't effectively teach the Bible unless you know what it says.	■ Determine that you will master the Scriptures. ■ Develop a Bible reading plan. ■ Organize your time so that you have time to study.
3	Make it a priority to apply the truth you learn to your own life.	■ Recognize that God's truth is for you first, and then for those you teach.
4	Master principles of communication and teaching.	■ Master a book such as Howard G. Hendricks' *Teaching to Change Lives*, so that you learn how to teach.[6]
5	Set up a continuing education program for yourself. Teaching is a lifelong ministry for those who have been assigned this gift.	■ Read books, study, attend seminars, take the time to prepare well. Take your gift of teaching seriously.

and consistent development. A dedicated disciple with the gift of teaching may rake leaves occasionally, but he or she will become really good at teaching.

Another abuse of spiritual gifts is to say, "I have only one. It makes no difference if I use it or not. Who would notice?" In the parable of the talents, the only person Jesus condemned was the one who did not use any gift at all. He made no distinction between the person with ten talents and the person with two.

Two other ways gifts can be abused are gift projection and gift exaltation.

Gift projection assumes that everyone else ought to have the same gift one has. Some gifts are so intense, and those who have them so dedicated and hard-driving, that they cannot understand why everyone doesn't do what they do. This is especially true with the gifts such as knowledge, faith, evangelism, and discernment of spirits. People with the gift of knowledge are tempted to say, "But everyone knows . . ." Those with the gift of faith tend to declare, "Where's *your* faith . . . " Those with the gift of evangelism often assume that people without this gift "don't work for the Lord." People with the gift of discernment of spirits tend to say, "But can't you see . . . ."

Gift exaltation is the attitude that a certain gift is a spiritual status symbol. Those without it are given the impression that they are second-class citizens of the kingdom. People who have power or sign gifts, or highly goal-oriented gifts like evangelism, often project this attitude, though they may not do so consciously.

One of the worst abuses of spiritual gifts is when people demand authority over others based on their gifts. People with gifts such as leadership or apostleship need to be particularly careful in this regard, because they are in high-profile positions. This is where a thorough understanding of servant leadership and the attitudes it embraces makes all the difference. Paul's counsel, "Do not think of yourself more highly than you ought, but rather think of yourself with sober judgment" is good advice (Rom. 12:3).

Another unfortunate abuse of spiritual gifts is self-appointment. There are people who dearly love to have certain church offices or positions, and in pursuit of those positions, proclaim that they have certain spiritual gifts, though there is no evidence that this is true. As we have emphasized many times, spiritual gifts are assigned by the Holy Spirit. They are not self-appointed.

Summary

Spiritual gifts must be identified and confirmed. Once this happens, they need to be used consistently and efficiently to the glory of God and for the advancement of His Kingdom.

Notes:

1. Ray C. Steadman, *Body Life*, revised edition (Ventura, Calif.: Regal Books, 1979), 150.
2. Roy Naden, *Your Spiritual Gifts: Making the Great Discovery* (Berrien Springs, Mich.: Instructional Product Development, 1989).
3. C. Peter Wagner, *Your Spiritual Gifts Can Help Your Church Grow*, revised edition (Ventura, Calif.: Regal Books, 1994).

TWELVE

Maximum Ministry

Once spiritual gifts are identified, the next step is to develop the gifts themselves and then use them to develop productive ministries.

Ministry and discipleship

The development of spiritual gifts is tied to discipleship. A disciple is a person who has been born again, joined the church, identified his or her spiritual gifts, accepted a role in the church compatible with those gifts, and is committed to fulfilling that role *without continual external motivation.*

Ellen White makes an interesting statement about discipleship. It may seem negative at first glance, but consider it carefully:

> It is not a virtue for men or women to excuse slow bungling at work of any character. The slow habits must be overcome. The man who is slow, and does his work at a disadvantage, is an unprofitable workman. . . . Dullness and ignorance are no virtue. . . . "Whatsoever thy hand findeth to do, do it with thy might." "Not slothful in business; fervent in spirit; serving the Lord."[1]

Having received a personal calling from the Lord through the assignment of spiritual gifts, it is up to you to put your gifts into practice on a regular basis. Throughout your lifetime, your principal roles in the church should be compatible with your spiritual gifts. There may be times when the needs of the church require performing a role or function that is outside of your regular ministry or not directly related to your particular gifts, but this should be a temporary situation. Most of the time you will function within the context of your primary spiritual gifts.

Developing your spiritual gifts

As we have seen, spiritual gifts are assigned by the Holy Spirit as part of the new-birth process. Once assigned, they enable and empower immediately. That means that people have the approval and authority of the Holy Spirit to work within the parameters of their spiritual gifts. They also receive a certain amount of understanding about how their gifts work, even if they have never intentionally identified them.

This initial empowerment, however, does not preclude the further development of the gifts through learning and practice. Spiritual gifts are developed through study, planning, and application. Study involves reading books and articles dealing with the area of your spiritual gifts and possibly observing someone with the same gifts in action. Paul's advice to Timothy is still good advice today: "Do your best to present yourself to God as one approved, a workman who does not need to be ashamed and who correctly handles the word of truth" (2 Tim. 2:15).

In chapter 11, we illustrated how the gift of teaching might be developed. Let's look at some other gifts. Consider, for example, the table on the following page concerning how to develop the gift of exhortation—or encouragement:

How to Develop the Gift of Exhortation

STEP	PROCEDURE	APPLICATION
1	Study the parts of the Bible that focus on application	■ Spend time learning how the Bible applies spiritual truth to everyday situations. ■ Apply these passages to your own life. ■ Keep a journal about these passages and your experiences with them. ■ Ask the Holy Spirit to help you recognize when these passages apply to a person's problems.
2	Study books and passages of the Bible that help you become sensitive to people's needs.	Example: Read the Psalms regularly, and notice: ■ The changing moods and experiences, even of the people who walked with the Lord. ■ How did the Lord meet those needs? ■ How can you use the various psalms to bring encouragement to those who face problems?
3	Study Ellen White materials that deal with how to meet human needs.	A study of the life of Jesus in *The Desire of Ages* is helpful. The two volumes entitled *Mind, Character, and Personality* are useful, as is *The Ministry of Healing.*
4	Memorize Scripture verses that apply to exhortation and encouragement.	Examples: Prov. 9:8; 10:17; 11:14; John 14:26; 16:13; 2 Cor. 1:3, 4; Heb. 10:24, 25.
5	Read and study other books and articles that have to do with this gift.	Examples: Morris Venden, *How Jesus Treated People; The Bible Promise Book;* and Oswald Chambers, *My Utmost for His Highest.*[2]
6	Develop an approach to helping people. Most of the time, people will come to you, because they will recognize that you have this gift.	■ People will question how you know that a particular scripture applies. ■ Be willing to be transparent and use your own walk with the Lord as an example.

How to develop the gift of faith

Dependence on God is the essence of this gift. By its very nature, the gift increases with its exercise, with the maturity of the believer with the gift, and with the growth of personal experience and knowledge of God. Suggestions for the development of this gift hinge on things that will increase one's knowledge, experience, and confidence in a mighty sovereign God and His willingness to honor faith (James 1:5, 6).

STEP	PROCEDURE	APPLICATION
1	Study passages of Scripture that focus on the gift of faith.	■ Do a word study on *faith*. ■ Study systematically the great miracles, signs, and wonders recorded in the Bible and how people reacted and related to them. ■ Notice the kinds of situations, barriers overcome, and final results when genuine faith was exercised.
2	Read information on faith in Ellen White's writings.	Examples:The miracles of Jesus that mention faith in *The Desire of Ages*. The chapter on faith in *Steps to Christ*.
3	Find a partner who has the gift of intercessory prayer.	This person will help focus your faith through prayer.
4	Memorize Bible passages that deal with faith.	Examples: Matt. 7:7-11; 21:21, 22; Mk. 9:23, 24; Jn. 14:12-14.

How to build a ministry

A ministry is any activity, outreach program, initiative, or ongoing enterprise in the church carried out by a person or group. For instance, a few ladies in one Adventist church decided to start a small bakery. They baked the bread in their ovens at home at night and sold it from a small storefront near the church during the day. The real purpose behind the bakery was the chance to engage people in conversation and share the gospel.

This bakery ministry produced results. A homeless young man happened to pass by one day at noon. Smelling the bread, he asked for some lunch. They gave it to him, and the next day he was back. They made a deal with him—food for work. As he worked his agreed-upon two hours, he heard the gospel story from the bakery ministry ladies. Not only did he become a church member, he eventually became the manager of the bakery. That's ministry!

Spiritual gifts are converted into ministries through initiative, organization, intercessory prayer, study, attendance at training sessions and seminars, and through use and practice. The Lord expects Christians to "professionalize" their ministry—to develop it to the best of their ability. "Whatever your hand finds to do, do it with all your might" (Eccl. 9:10) is the watchword for developing ministries.

Ministries may be one-person types, small-group oriented, needs oriented, or large-group oriented. They may be service, administrative, or counseling ministries. Some fall into the category of pastoral care. Church offices such as elder and deacon fall into larger categories of leadership or service.

Organization and teamwork

Make sure your ministry is well organized and has an adequate and dedicated team running it. Ministries don't function in a vacuum, and they don't always produce immediate results. Ministries are long-term investments that eventually pay off in consistent growth in spiritual maturity, converts to the church, and the development of even more ministries that contribute to a consistent growth cycle.

While your ministry will originally be built around your particular spiritual gifts, you usually end up working with other people whose gifts complement your own. For instance, if your gift is evangelism, you may specialize in home Bible studies. At some point, however, your interested persons will come to the church. You then need people with gifts of hospitality to greet them, with gifts of teaching to teach them, and gifts of pastoring to confirm them in the faith. That's how the body life, or unity, principle works (Rom. 12:4).[2]

Building blocks for ministry

There are five basic building blocks for effective ministry:

1. Ascertain needs.
2. Target the ministry.
3. Build a ministry team.
4. Design a specific plan of action.
5. Develop a keen sense of how the ministry relates to the total church strategy.

Building block 1: Ascertain needs

Both internal and external needs should be ascertained. Internally, review church membership records and list the various types of needs such as single parents, overachievers, nonmember spouses, etc.—not necessarily by people's names, but by the number of such people in the church family. If a significant number who fit a category are in the congregation, and there is no specific ministry for them, they may be a target group that matches your particualr spiritual gifts.

For the community, use a survey sheet or demographic data to gather information useful in targeting a ministry.

Building block 2: Target a ministry

Ministries need to focus on an issue, group of people, or a particular need. The target is discovered through the research done under step 1, talking with people in the church, brainstorming with friends and associates, and through the leading of the Holy Spirit. For instance, if you have the gift of missionary, the Lord may lead you to develop a ministry among a previously unrecognized or unentered people group within your sphere of influence.

Building block 3: Put together a ministry team

Individual spiritual gifts rarely function as isolated entities. They are designed to function in conjunction with other gifts. That is why the Holy Spirit assigns various gifts to people and to church congregations. As you develop your gift-based ministry, you will need to develop cooperative ventures with other people. This is what brings unity to the church and enhances creativity and initiative.

The chart below outlines some of the elements needed in cooperative ventures, as spiritual gifts become the basis for ministries in the church:

SKILLS NEEDED	GIFTS OR HELPS NEEDED
People skills	What people skills will you need to carry out this ministry? Make a list of the skills you will need and the people you can recruit who have those skills.
Training	What kind of training will the people who work with you need? Make a list of the type of training needed and how and where it can be obtained.
Support Groups	What kind of support groups do you need to help you make your ministry a success? Find some people who will counterbalance your temperament. For instance, if you tend to get discouraged easily, find someone with the gift of faith and someone with the gift of pastoring for your support group.
Resource Support	What kind of resource support do you need? For instance, if you don't like to study and do research, find someone else to do this part of the ministry. You may also need to find someone who can give financial support to your ministry.

As an example, ministries that deal with small groups, seminar programs, Branch Sabbath Schools, etc. need the team outlined in the table on the following page:

TEAM MEMBER	SPIRITUAL GIFTS	ROLE
Ministry coordinator	Leadership and Administration	The ministry coordinator is the group administrator: ■ Organizes the team ■ Keeps it together ■ Keeps it moving ■ Is able to communicate with the target audience
Clerical assistant	Administration and Helps	The clerical assistant takes care of the physical arrangements for the ministry meetings and handles the multitude of details that arises. ■ Makes phone calls ■ Does scheduling ■ Handles purchases ■ Takes care of paperwork ■ Sets up equipment ■ Distributes advertising
Hospitality coordinator	Hospitality	The hospitality coordinator is the social director of the team. This person knows how to make people feel comfortable and welcome. ■ Chats with people ■ Gets to know attendees ■ Answers questions ■ Organizes visitation
Support liaison	This person represents the unity factor (Rom. 12:4)	This person functions as the liaison and advocate for the ministry to the church board, etc. Could be from the pastoral staff—or an elder.
Prayer leader	Intercessory prayer, Pastoring	Leads out in intercessory prayer. This is the ministry's "pastor," who looks out for the spiritual welfare of the ministry members and those who are served by the ministry.

Recruiting volunteers

Besides the leadership core, the ministry will need additional volunteers. The ministry team will usually recruit its own volunteers. Often they are friends and relatives of people on the team. Volunteers work until the job they volunteered for is done. Then they have to be recruited again if needed. They usually look for five specific things before they decide to become involved:

1. Specific tasks with clearly defined limits.
2. Short terms in office.
3. Plenty of people power to use in attaining the goal.
4. Simple, direct feedback about how they are doing.
5. Lots of affirmation.

Building block 4: Put together a plan of action

The plan of action consists of the actual details of a ministry. It is the packaging of the ministry in concrete terms. Many ministries fail because they just start and hope for the best without a plan of action. Use the following to develop an operational plan for your ministry:

Base of operations: Where will your base of operations be? Your home, the church? Will you need to rent a building or office? Where will you meet?

Building a schedule: How often will you meet? Does everyone helping you have to be there all the time? Who will help you organize this schedule?

How will you go about starting your ministry? With whom do you need to talk? What authorizations will you need?

Developing a time-line for your ministry. It usually takes about three months to plan and organize a new ministry. If you try to do it faster, something will be left out, and the project will probably fail. Don't be impatient. Do it once and do it right. Use a chart to indicate what you expect to accomplish in three months, one year, and long-term.

Develop a document that includes:

1. A specific description of the needs this ministry will meet.
2. A statement of the objectives of the ministry, including the expected outcomes.
3. A list of the ministry coordinator and team members.
4. A program design.
5. An indication of where the ministry will meet.
6. The time of year when it will meet.
7. A list of the resources available.
8. A budget.
9. A starting date.

Building block 5: Design a plan for integrating new members

This step deals with integrating new members into the congregation. If you are fortunate enough to belong to a church that practices true Christian *koinonia*, this step will be much easier. All too many congregations, however, are hard to "get into." New members are often locked out by psychological attitudes and body language that clearly indicates to them that they are not wanted, even if the people who do this don't know they are doing it.

Those working in your ministry must take the initiative in integrating the people with whom you are working into the congregation. If you turn them loose on their own, they will probably be lost rather quickly. *Studies show that when people initially attend church, you have thirty seconds to make a good impression, the first two minutes are crucial, and within five minutes they will have made a fairly firm decision about the church.*

Your ministry team should:

■ Take the people to church activities—don't send them on their own. Be careful who you introduce them to! Keep them away from the emotionally unstable and questionable elements of the congregation. Don't let them fall into the clutches of people who immediately want to indoctrinate them in their particular lifestyle, point of view, or theological hobby horse.

Don't introduce doctors, for instance, to the chronically ill member who will immediately ask for "free" medical advice.

■ Show them through the building and orient them on the activities that take place.

■ Orient them to the vocabulary they will hear. For instance, a manager may be disturbed hearing people talking about the "union," assuming they mean "labor union."

Summary

The Holy Spirit's purpose in assigning spiritual gifts is that a person's primary gifts become the framework for lifelong ministry. There are many types of activities that fit gifts, but planning and organization are essential for the success of a ministry. It is each person's responsibility to learn how to carry out his or her ministry effectively and proficiently. Part of that training includes learning how to motivate—and to use resources. Cooperative ventures with other people are also important.

Notes:

1. Ellen G. White, *Fundamentals of Christian Education*, 316.
2. Information on building ministries is also available in expanded form in a workbook entitled *Building Effective Ministries: A Planning Guide*. It can be obtained through many conferences and divisions throughout the world as well as from AdventSource, The North American Division distribution center.

THIRTEEN

Putting the Right People in the Right Place for the Right Reasons

Just as individual members have spiritual gift mixes, so congregations also have mixtures of gifts. The ministries a congregation can efficiently and effectively carry out depend to a great extent on the mixture of gifts in that congregation. Intentionally incorporating spiritual giftedness into the organizational system of the congregation will enhance the church's ability to fulfill its mission.

Seventh-day Adventist churches are usually organized around officers (elders, deacons, deaconesses, clerks, and treasurers) and departments (Sabbath School, Adventist Youth, etc.). These positions are filled by the annual nominating committee, usually following the list outlined in the *Church Manual*.

According to the *Church Manual*, the nominating committee has a twofold purpose: (1) to give careful study to the needs of the church, and (2) to make careful inquiry into the fitness of members to serve.

Often the phrase "fitness to serve" is overlooked or ignored by nominating committees. Sometimes, "fitness to serve" is understood to mean that the nominating committee must make a judgment call regarding an individual's spiritual maturity, or that it must at least assure the church that a nominee's life shows no visible signs of unbecoming conduct. Too often, however, "fitness to serve" is restricted to a person's availability, seniority, or social standing.

"Fitness to serve" ought to include, however, the identifiable spiritual giftedness of those who will be responsible for carrying out the various activities of the church.

Identifying your church's spiritual gift mix

Once individual members identify their gifts and ministries, a church can categorize its primary and secondary combinations of gifts by ranking the gifts of the members. A church can then develop programs and projects that utilize the giftedness of its members.

This corporate giftedness may change as members come and go. An annual evaluation of giftedness as part of the nominating committee process will indicate the changes that have taken place. Once a congregation has been surveyed for spiritual giftedness, all you need is a yearly update of new and/or formerly nonparticipating members to keep your corporate-giftedness information up to date.

Essential gift combinations

There are four sets of gifts that are always needed, and will, almost always, appear in the church. If one of these sets of gifts is missing, the church must pray earnestly that the Lord will provide it, either by calling someone within the church or sending someone with that gift to the church.

- Set one: gifts of evangelism
- Set two: gifts of leadership and administration
- Set three: gifts of pastoring and hospitality
- Set four: gifts of teaching

Gifts of evangelism enhance the church's ability to contact people and bring in new converts. Gifts of leadership and administration ensure forward-looking vision and organization in the church's program. Gifts of pastoring and hospitality assure adequate nurture and fellowship, while gifts of teaching guarantee knowledge and understanding of the church's theology and message.

Support gifts such as helps, giving, and service are usually found in all congregations, but they need to be intentionally organized and systematized. The gift of exhortation or encouragement is usually practiced spontaneously by individual members. It may also be used systematically through the establishment of a peer counseling system in the church.

Intercessory prayer is a core ministry that ought to be functioning at all times. It is the place where all gifted persons or groups of persons can go for prayer support for their ministries.

Tasks and spiritual gifts

When Paul outlined a philosophy of ministry built around spiritual gifts, there were no church buildings to maintain, no zoning laws to struggle with, no building codes or fire inspections, no denominational organizations, no income tax laws or medical plans, no monthly treasurer's reports. There were few of the multitude of church "tasks" that keep congregations busy today. Spiritual gifts were focused on ministry, primarily church planting and expansion growth.

Sometimes, a person may have a mixture of gifts that includes secondary gifts that fit certain church tasks but which do not form part of the person's primary ministry choice. The Lord will amplify the secondary gifts for the good of the kingdom and confirm and bless abundantly the person's ministry. This, however, should be a temporary situation until someone with a more appropriate mixture of gifts appears on the scene.

Spiritual gifts and nurture

All churches need a nurture system to incorporate new members into the church and care for the needs of the congregation. This is where the "one another" system comes into play.

The Greek word translated "one another" is used seventy-six times in the New Testament. The uses of this word give a picture of what could be called the corporate Christian personality of a local church. (See the chart on page 59 that groups these statements into four categories: interrelationships, mutual edification, mutual service, and negative "one anothers." These categories represent an interdependent ministry in which individual members develop Christian personalities (Gal. 5:22) for the benefit of all. It includes the use of spiritual gifts and the practice of upbuilding the entire church body. The system could be called "reciprocal living."

One of the first steps in utilizing spiritual gifts on the corporate congregational level should be a teaching/preaching design that intentionally motivates the congregation to practice these reciprocal relationships. This is what brings unity to the church body in the sense that Paul talked about it in 1 Cor. 12 and Rom. 12. Notice some examples of how reciprocal living and spiritual gifts compliment each other:

SPIRITUAL GIFT	RECIPROCAL LIVING
Teaching	"Teach one another" — Col. 3:16
Exhortation / encouragement	"Exhort one another" — 1 Thess. 5:11
Faith	"Pray for one another" — James 5:16
Prophecy	"Build up one another" — Rom. 14:19
Helps	"Serve one another" — Gal. 5:13, 14

If these reciprocal commands were followed, there would be no judging of other people's characters. There would be no unkind criticism or envy of others. There would be mutual respect for all people. Your congregation would be a little bit of heaven on earth.

Organizing a spiritually gifted ministry system

Organizing this type of leadership approach requires a combination of adept administration and knowledge of the mixture of spiritual gifts in the congregation.

The first step is to organize a process that will furnish the nominating committee with the information it needs to assign people to positions that match their mixture of gifts. (See chart on page 141.)

Prayer and Planning Commission

Form a Prayer and Planning Commission that will seek, through prayer, careful study, and organization, the will and blessing of the Lord in discovering and meeting the needs of the church and the community. The commission will plan ministries that match the individual and corporate gift mixtures, with the needs of the church and the community.

The pastor usually leads the Prayer and Planning Commission, though with experience and training, other members may lead out. Members of the commission may choose to be on one of three task forces: Needs of the Church, Needs of the Community, or Gifts and Ministries of the Church. Each task force will choose its own leadership, and the pastor will act as an advisor.

The process takes about five weeks, organized as illustrated in the chart at the top of the next page.

The assignment of the *Gifts and Ministries Task Force* is to update the church's database of individual spiritual gifts. Experience teaches that a general spiritual-gifts inventory of the entire congregation once every two years is usually adequate. An annual update will help new members and members who have not previously done so to identify their gifts. This task force will also evaluate the congregation's corporate mixture of gifts. If a specific need exists with no gifts to fill it, the intercessory prayer ministry of the church will add this to its list of petitions, asking the Lord to fill the need.

WEEK 1	WEEK 2	WEEK 3	WEEK 4	WEEK 5
Organize		**Survey and Interpret**		**Final Planning Session**
■ Overview of purpose ■ Form task forces ■ Choose leaders ■ Discuss surveys and procedures		■ Take surveys ■ Compile results		■ Compile report for nominating committee

The *Needs of the Church Task Force* interviews the leadership of existing ministries to see if additional help is needed and surveys the membership regarding existing activities and the church's overall program.

The *Needs of the Community Task Force* will survey the community and update demographic data. There are many community-survey documents available from your Adventist Book Center or conference office.

As the materials come in, the Prayer and Planning Commission will compile the data and prepare a questionnaire for the nominating committee, similar to the sample beginning below. This questionnaire will guide the committee in filling new positions, taking spiritual gifts into account as part of the process.

Job Description

Position:

Task/responsibilities:

Communication links:

Reports to:

Gets reports from:

Works closely with:

Gifts required Skills required

Tenure (normal): ______Weeks/months/years

Standard of performance:

Comments:

The following list is a sample of gifts that match various ministries and functions in a church:

1. Sabbath School teacher—teaching, knowledge
2. Evangelism team—the gift of evangelist, plus cognate gifts:
3. Visitation—evangelist, exhortation
4. Door-to-door—evangelist
5. Bible studies—evangelist, teaching
6. Team leader—evangelist, administration
7. Church elder—pastor, exhortation, leadership, teaching, administration.
8. Finance committee—administration, wisdom.
9. Youth ministry—exhortation, pastor, hospitality, leadership.

10. Sabbath School superintendent—administration, leadership.
11. Church secretary—helps, administration.
12. Nursery attendant—service, mercy.
13. Deacon or deaconess—service, helps, mercy.
14. Head deacon/deaconess—administration, service.

That's a lot of work!

Yes, it is. Whether it is worth it or not, or whether or not your church is willing to take the time to do it, depends on the level of discipleship of your congregation. It is more work when the system is first established than when it is in place. Once a system like this is functioning, it doesn't take as much time to maintain it.

Summary

Spiritual gifts can be effectively used as part of the life of the church, through careful planning and by establishing a system in the church that intentionally takes them into account. By putting the right people in the right place for the right reasons, your church's ministry will be more effective in advancing the cause of the kingdom.

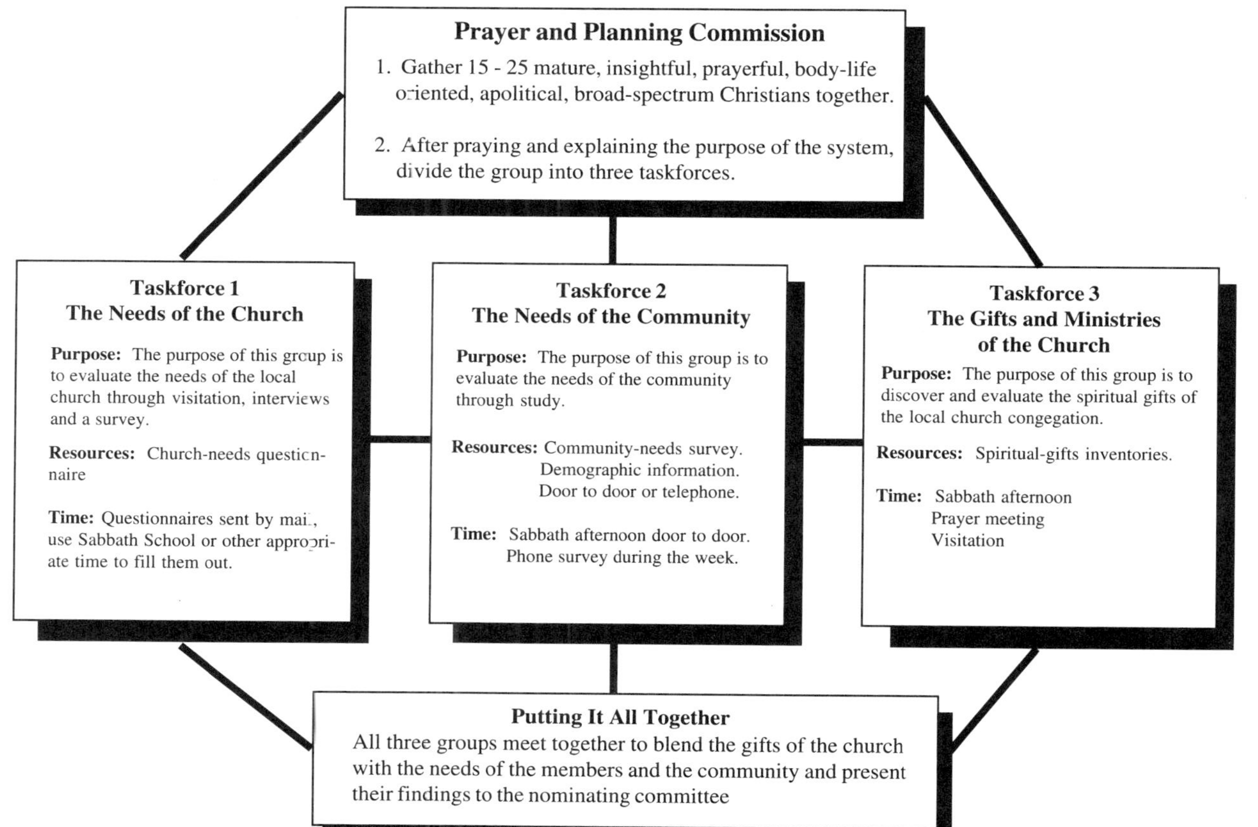
Prayer and Planning Commission
1. Gather 15 - 25 mature, insightful, prayerful, body-life oriented, apolitical, broad-spectrum Christians together.
2. After praying and explaining the purpose of the system, divide the group into three taskforces.
Taskforce 1
The Needs of the Church
Purpose: The purpose of this group is to evaluate the needs of the local church through visitation, interviews and a survey.
Resources: Church-needs questionnaire
Time: Questionnaires sent by mail, use Sabbath School or other appropriate time to fill them out.
Taskforce 2
The Needs of the Community
Purpose: The purpose of this group is to evaluate the needs of the community through study.
Resources: Community-needs survey.
Demographic information.
Door to door or telephone.
Time: Sabbath afternoon door to door.
Phone survey during the week.
Taskforce 3
The Gifts and Ministries of the Church
Purpose: The purpose of this group is to discover and evaluate the spiritual gifts of the local church congegation.
Resources: Spiritual-gifts inventories.
Time: Sabbath afternoon
Prayer meeting
Visitation
Putting It All Together
All three groups meet together to blend the gifts of the church with the needs of the members and the community and present their findings to the nominating committee